Problems of the
Developing Nations

Problems of the

Developing Nations

Readings and Case Studies

LEWIS P. FICKETT, JR.

Mary Washington College of the University of Virginia

164

THOMAS Y. CROWELL COMPANY

New York / Established 1834

To Karin and Sybil

with much love

Preface

This book is designed to fill the need for a basic undergraduate text on the problems of the developing nations. To this end, I have selected what I believe to be the best available readings on the four fundamental aspects of the developmental process—the sociological, the economic, the military, and the political. In addition, I have applied the concepts presented in the introductory readings to six major developing countries—Algeria, Tunisia, India, Pakistan, Indonesia, and Thailand.

These case studies are not, of course, intended to be definitive analyses of the countries concerned. Rather, I have pinpointed certain major problems, common to all developing nations, and have illustrated by comparison the approaches taken by these nations in solving their problems. Thus, a student, after completing this text, should have acquired an adequate theoretical and practical foundation for understanding the developmental process.

I want to express my deep appreciation to my colleagues, Dr. Almont Lindsay and Dr. Carrol Quenzel, for reading portions of the manuscript and offering many helpful suggestions; to Miss Marguerite Carder and the Mary Washington College Library staff for their cheerful assistance; to Chancellor Grellet Simpson for his kindness in authorizing adequate secretarial assistance; and, of course, to my wife for her inspiration, cooperation, and unstinting efforts to make the project a reality.

L. P. F.

Fredericksburg, Virginia
October, 1965

Contents

1 The Challenge of Development

Development, in its broadest sense, is that great historical process by which societies have evolved from the primitive tribal states of prehistory to the complex, mature, industrial societies of today. What we are concerned with here is only the most recent stage of that process—the attempt of the many peoples and nations who were left behind in the historical race to modernize themselves.

Almost as late as a generation ago the less developed countries of today were a concern of very low priority. Most of them were at that time under some form of European colonial administration. A few, such as Thailand and Ethiopia, retained a precarious independence as buffer states between rival colonial powers.

World War II radically changed this situation. Perhaps the most profound and lasting result of the war was the fact that it unleashed the explosive power of nationalism, which for the most part had been slumbering throughout the vast reaches of the underdeveloped areas of the world. The war stripped the "superman" aura from the colonial overlord, and in so doing, it often revealed him in defeat as nothing more than a paper tiger. In addition, some of the wartime invaders often rekindled flickering nationalist movements by establishing them as puppet governments, as the Japanese did in the Philippines and Indonesia. The war also provided a great impetus to the economic development of such areas because of the wartime needs of either the mother or the occupying countries.

The postwar impact of the new nationalism had two major manifestations: first, the achievement of national independence, and second, the attempt to satisfy the "revolution of rising expectations."

The first of these usually occasioned the launching of a revolutionary movement and the waging of some form of warfare against the respective colonial power, except when the colonial power gracefully withdrew, as the British sometimes did. Whatever the means, however, the objective was relatively clear-cut, the strategy obvious. As a result most of the former colonial areas are now free and have acquired the basic prerogatives of sovereignty.

The second manifestation of this postwar phenomenon has opened a Pandora's box of new problems. How can this "revolution" in material aspirations be satisfied? What is the key to the developmental process? And more important to the nations of the West, which system of values and techniques—the Communist system or a democratic system—is going to seem more desirable to these newly independent peoples? For it is obvious that the long-term survival of the West's system is going to be dependent in large measure upon its acceptability to the great majority of the world's people, who live in the so-called "underdeveloped areas." This, then, is the challenge of development from the Western point of view— to make our system of values and techniques the most attractive.

The Marshall Plan Fallacy

Secretary of State George C. Marshall's initiative in June 1947 caused the United States to undertake an unprecedented, massive program of economic assistance to the war-shattered countries of Western Europe. This program, which extended over four years and cost over $13 billion, was a triumphant success. The free nations of Western Europe not only recovered and rebuilt the foundations of their societies, but were enabled as well to achieve new standards of wealth and unity.

This "success story" led unfortunately to the acceptance of a fallacy: since Western Europe has enjoyed such spectacular economic progress as a consequence of American economic assistance, similar results can be achieved by providing similar aid to the less developed areas of the world. This fallacy inspired President Harry S. Truman's Point Four Program, which was designed to provide technical assistance to the underdeveloped areas. In fact, however, the Marshall Plan experience emphasized a distinction of great importance in the administration of foreign aid—a distinction between *situations in which external assistance is a necessary and sufficient condition for economic development and situations in which it is a necessary but not a sufficient condition.*[1] At the end of World War II the countries of Western Europe possessed all the requirements for recovery and continued development except the command over sufficient foreign exchange to replenish their stocks of working capital, to repair and replace destroyed production facilities, and to make it possible to restore the flow of intra-European trade. This the Marshall Plan provided.

What the United States overlooked in its generous enthusiasm was the tremendous number of discrepancies between the advanced economies of Western Europe and those of the less developed nations. The Marshall Plan served merely as a powerful catalyst which stimulated and released the tremendous potential inherent in the mature industrial societies of Western Europe. Unfortunately such potential does not yet exist in most of the underdeveloped areas of the world. In fact, the so-called success stories of our foreign aid program—Japan, Israel, Nationalist China—belong to that first category of nations, those in which external assistance was both a necessary and a sufficient condition for economic development.[2] In other areas—India, Nigeria, Colombia, for example—substantial progress has been achieved, but the drive to attain self-generating growth is far from over.[3] In still other areas external assistance finances nothing more than survey or hold-the-line programs which only scratch the surface of massive economic problems.

Development: An Uncharted Sea

"In the 'brave new world' of President Truman's Point Four, all things seemed possible. Technological assistance was going to lift

[1] Edward S. Mason, *Foreign Aid and Foreign Policy* (New York: Harper and Row, 1964), p. 38.
[2] Ibid., p. 39.   [3] Ibid.

the underdeveloped world by its bootstraps without the need for large flows of capital. When these hopes were disappointed, there appeared on the scene the econometricians brandishing their savings ratios and capital-output coefficients. . . . These experts too are now somewhat less vocal."[4]

Still later in the postwar period, great emphasis was placed upon the construction of what was called "infrastructure," that is, such basic sinews of modern industry and communications as highways, ports, industrial plants, and telecommunications facilities.

Now we are beginning to appreciate that the underdeveloped world cannot "simply import the industrial revolution from abroad, uncrate it like a piece of machinery, and set it in motion."[5] We are realizing that economic development requires such *institutions, habits, incentives,* and *motivations* that the inputs necessary to a continuous increase in output will be self-generating.[6] In some underdeveloped countries it is difficult to visualize how the initial inputs necessary to increased outputs are to be generated. In some areas material improvement does not rank high in the scale of values accepted by the population. In others exploitative landowners siphon off the profits, taking away the vital increments needed for future growth. In still other areas corrupt governments and governmental officials sidetrack or block needed reforms. In short, it is beginning to be realized that "in various parts of the underdeveloped world the prospects for economic growth will not become particularly bright until there are some rather profound changes in human motivations and values and in the socio-political structure."[7]

What are some of these "profound changes" that are required? Understandably the requirements will vary with the country and its current situation. In certain countries "it may be the introduction of policies conducive to monetary stabilization and a viable exchange rate. In others, it may be self-help measures designed to increase the contribution of local resources to development."[8] In some, various social reforms, including land reform, may be called

---

[4] Ibid., p. 22.
[5] Edward S. Mason, "The Planning of Development," *Technology and Economic Development* (New York: Knopf, 1963), p. 181.
[6] Ibid., p. 182.   [7] Ibid., p. 183.   [8] Ibid.

for. Or, of course, a combination of several or all of these measures may be required. There is clearly no universal blueprint that can be used by us. We must experiment and learn by our experiences. Above all, we must not be doctrinaire or ethnocentric in our approach.

Recent Trends in Developmental Theory

With the experience acquired during the last fifteen years, we can make certain general observations about the developmental process.

First, and perhaps most important, it should be acknowledged that economic development is not primarily an economic process but rather a political and a social process.[9] The simple offering of technical know-how as provided for in the original Point Four Program was not enough. Economic development required not merely capital and technology; "it is concerned with the shaping of attitudes, and the creation, forcibly or otherwise, of workable institutional structures."[10] It demands the acquisition of new skills, new habits, new institutions—all of which require far-reaching social change, and this social change, in turn, requires for its inception the mobilization of powerful political energies.

This principle has required a shift in our foreign aid program from the provision of tools and equipment to an emphasis upon the development of human resources such as health, basic education, and technical skills. Moreover, there has developed concomitantly an emphasis by indigenous political leaders upon the need for altering community attitudes which have slowed the pace of modernization. A recent example of this was the campaign by President Habib Bourguiba of Tunisia to persuade his people to forego the long fast required by the Moslem feast of Ramadan.

Second, we are gradually realizing that the political and social changes required for economic development are apt to be revolutionary in nature.[11] Nowhere is this more obvious than in Latin

[9] Robert L. Heilbroner, *The Great Ascent* (New York: Harper and Row, 1963), p. 16.
[10] Ibid.   [11] Ibid., p. 17.

5

America. To date, only three countries in this vast area have carried out a significant land reform program—Bolivia, Cuba, and Mexico. In each of these instances, it is sad but important to note, the land reform was the consequence not of an enlightened evolutionary movement but rather of a bloody and prolonged revolution. The experiences of Iran and Venezuela in this connection are still too limited to provide examples to the contrary. In other words, we must face the fact that the drastic, rapid, and painful redistribution of power which took place during the French and Russian revolutions is more likely to represent the norm of development than is our own national experience.

Third, it is important to recognize that the price of development is apt to be political and economic authoritarianism.[12] While the pattern will vary from country to country, the inherent stresses of development—social friction, universal transformation of institutions, the arduousness of the prospect—are likely to result in highly centralized control. Strong-man governments and collectivistic economic techniques are likely to accompany development in many backward areas as the necessary conditions for sustaining the great effort required.

Some commentators are even more pessimistic and contend that the developing nations must forswear political democracy and follow single-minded, harsh, even fanatic leaderships zealously dedicated to genuine cultural and social revolutions such as Kemal Ataturk achieved in Turkey.[13] Others believe that only political democracy can breach the dam of tradition and release the pent-up aspirations, talents, and drives of countless individuals essential to modernization.[14] It is important, however, to note that even these optimists have in mind a tutelary type of democracy, as exemplified and practiced by the late Prime Minister Jawaharlal Nehru of India.

If we accept these generalizations as reasonable reflections of the present realities of development in the less developed countries,

[12] Ibid., p. 20.

[13] I. R. Sinai, *The Challenge of Modernisation* (New York: Norton, 1964).

[14] William McCord, *The Springtime of Freedom* (New York: Oxford Univ. Press, 1965).

is it not desirable to attempt to develop a theory of transition for these newly independent states? Can we not seek to develop or to recognize a variant of traditional democracy which would constitute for these new states a "halfway house" between the fatalistic acceptance of totalitarianism and the frustration created by failure to achieve Western democracy in them? Neal Riemer provided us with the outline of such a possible compromise:

1. If strong-man rule seems a current need, can theory and practice in the new states recognize and facilitate the emergence of at least a constitutional dictatorship, a practice not unknown in the traditional theory and practice of the West? . . .

2. If a single party system seems currently indispensable in most of the new states, can theory and practice recognize and encourage its democratic possibilities? . . .

3. If military rule seems essential in some of the new states for short periods of time in order to preserve unity, and fight against corruption, or if the military is heavily relied upon to support the national leadership, can theory and practice recognize and stimulate the armed forces' modernizing and democratic potential? . . .

4. If a large measure of state planning seems obligatory for economic and social advance, can theory and practice recognize and encourage the emergence of a sane welfare state based upon a sound "mixed economy" wherein basic freedoms are preserved, abuse of power guarded against, planning blunders minimized, efficient administration maximized, and ample room left for local initiatives and entrepreneurial innovation?[15]

These are some of the possibilities which we will explore in this book.

SELECTED BIBLIOGRAPHY

ALMOND, GABRIEL, and JAMES COLEMAN. *The Politics of the Developing Areas*. Princeton, N.J.: Princeton Univ. Press, 1960.

[15] Neal Riemer, "Democratic Theory and the New States: The Dilemma of Transition" (p. 9 of unpublished paper presented at the Annual Meeting of the American Political Science Association, Chicago, Ill., September 9–12, 1964).

HEILBRONER, R. L. *The Great Ascent.* New York: Harper and Row, 1963.

MC CORD, WILLIAM. *The Springtime of Freedom.* New York: Oxford Univ. Press, 1965.

MILLIKAN, M. F., and D. L. M. BLACKMER, eds. *The Emerging Nations.* Boston: Little, Brown, 1961.

PYE, L. W. *Politics, Personality and Nation Building.* New Haven, Conn.: Yale Univ. Press, 1962.

ROSTOW, W. W. *The Stages of Economic Growth.* London: Cambridge Univ. Press, 1960.

WARD, BARBARA. *The Rich Nations and the Poor Nations.* New York: Norton, 1962.

Introductory Readings

2 The Sociological Aspects

In recent years there has developed an increasing recognition of the mutual dependence between changes in economic activity and organization and changes in social structure. Taken in its most unsophisticated form, this interrelationship has usually been expressed as a very simple premise: economic development is only possible if the social relations of an underdeveloped country are reformed so as to resemble those of Western capitalistic countries. Bert Hoselitz interprets this viewpoint as concluding "that if any successful development is to take place, the countries of Asia, Africa, and Latin America will have to adopt social institutions and even social values resembling those of the West. In somewhat more down-to-earth terms they will all have to become little Americas."

While the premise may contain a considerable amount of truth, it must be pointed out that the Marxian theory of economic and social development, when stripped of its purely political appendages, is closely analogous. Basically, Marxian theory postulates a single-line process of social and economic development, and states that with only minor deviations from the postulate all societies must go through analogous transformations of social structure in order to reach higher levels of productivity and economic organization. Thus these two theories of the developmental process are (1) analogous in their recognition of the necessity for sweeping changes in the social values and institutions of the less developed countries and (2) in vigorous competition for consideration and adoption by such countries.

Regardless of which system or combination each of the less developed countries chooses, the choice will inevitably require tremendous disruption of traditional patterns of life. This disruption will, in turn, meet considerable resistance in all of the basic areas affected by change—politics, economics, and social structure. The first selection deals with the principal aspects of this vital process of change. The second selection focuses on the key importance of both agricultural reform and community development in the less developed areas of the world.

Resistance and Conflict in the Modernization Process

edited by MAX F. MILLIKAN and DONALD L. M. BLACKMER

It is one thing for a traditional society to be moved toward change by internal factors or to experience the intrusion of modern elements which in favorable circumstances set in motion new dynamic trends. It is quite a different matter for such a society to achieve a working modern system which moves toward constructive objectives by increasingly democratic means. Before a modern society can be achieved—before the modern elements within a traditional society can become not only dominant but constructive—a succession of profound changes must take place; for any established society has deeply rooted characteristics which yield only reluctantly, with pain and the passage of time, and only to strong and persistent pressure for change.

Thus time is required for the social structure to be altered, for new political attitudes and institutions to be created and consolidated, for the creation of the skills and habits and institutions on

SOURCE: Reprinted from *The Emerging Nations: Their Growth and United States Foreign Policy*, edited by Max F. Millikan and Donald L. M. Blackmer, by permission of Little, Brown and Company. Copyright © 1961, Massachusetts Institute of Technology. All rights reserved. No part of this book may be reproduced in any form without permission in writing from the publisher.

which capital formation depends. Above all, time must pass for new generations to succeed one another, each finding the environment, techniques, and goals of modernization a bit more familiar and ac-ceptable.

Historical experience indicates that no society ever simply aban-dons its traditional culture. On the contrary, the old culture almost always leaves permanent and significant marks of continuity on the fully modernized society. Nevertheless, the traditional culture must undergo drastic alteration. It is thus of the very nature of the modernizing process that at every step of the way the impulses mak-ing for modernization are in active contention with powerful forces tending to retard and to frustrate the transformation of the tradi-tional society into full constructive modernity. There is nothing which decrees that the forces of modernization will win eventual or automatic victory. The interplay between the new hopes and the old ways may yield bloody civil conflict susceptible to exploitation by external powers; there may be efforts to channel the moderniza-tion process into disruptive foreign adventures; the society's politics may be seized by dictators who exploit popular frustrations and the inevitable looseness of the transitional period for their own purposes.

In any case, there are three principal areas in which elements of resistance must be overcome if the modernization of a traditional society is to be carried through successfully: politics, economics, and social structure. The underlying requirement for change in these areas is the modernization of attitudes. Modernity is a style of life. The ensemble of behaviors that compose the modern style is given its coherence by a frame of mind—toward the here and hereafter, toward permanence and change, toward oneself and one's fellow-men. We shall undertake to characterize the modern perspective more fully later in this chapter.

Politically, the people must come to accept new forms for the organization of power based on the creation of a minimally effective national government. The balance of social and political power must shift from the village to the city, from the tasks and virtues of agri-cultural life to those of commerce, industry, and modern administra-tion. The people must begin—in a process with many difficult stages—to judge politics and politicians in terms of policies rather than merely in terms of inherited status or personality; and, if the goal is democracy, they must develop forms for transferring power by registering consent. Much energy and attention must be devoted to overcoming residues of traditional political authority which cannot be harnessed constructively to the purposes of the new national government. Examples are the sects in South Vietnam, the Indian princes, the Chinese war lords, the African tribal leaders. The new government must also develop a core of technically trained men capable of maintaining order, collecting taxes, and organizing the staff work required for the inevitably substantial role of government in the economy and in the educational process. If it is to survive, the new government must also demonstrate effective leadership in establishing programs to promote the new aspirations which modernization tends to instill in the minds of various groups of citizens. Means of communication must be developed between the government and its citizens to convey to them that the national goals being pursued are ones they would sanction.

Political development thus must contend with vested power derived from the traditional society, with a lack of trained men, with a low literacy rate and a lack of other facilities permitting persuasive mass communication, with loyalties limited largely to traditional groups rather than to the nation as a whole, and with the absence of a widespread sense that the new national government is an appropriate vehicle for furthering popular goals. In dealing with these problems many occasions will arise for frustration and backsliding, many ways in which political life may be diverted to sterile or disruptive goals. The Communist appeal to the underdeveloped areas is designed to exploit precisely these possibilities.

Economically, the society must achieve a situation where it regularly saves and productively invests a sufficient volume of its resources, and regularly adopts new ways of doing things. The growth of the national economy must begin to outpace population increase so that continuing economic growth can become a normal condition, a process which in itself involves every dimension of the society and many sectors of the economy.

Resistance to modernization may take the form of certain basic initial economic weaknesses. A very considerable expansion must take place in the number of modern men and institutions, as well as in physical capital, before sustained growth is possible at rates that substantially outstrip population increase. To achieve basic economic change, men must cease to regard the physical world as fixed. They must learn that it is capable of being understood and manipulated in terms of stable and logical rules which men can master. Above all, they must desire to use their energies in manipulating the physical world rather than regard such an activity as demeaning and distasteful. But such a change in attitude is not enough. Before a society's economy can grow regularly at a rate higher than its population increase, large numbers of men must be trained in specialized techniques; and these men must learn to apply systematically and progressively to the production of goods and services what modern science and technology have created. The society must come to desire to use its surplus above minimum consumption not for high living for a few, nor for war, nor for traditional monuments, but for productive investments. Moreover, the industrial process itself requires that important nonindustrial sectors be developed: notably, social overhead capital, agriculture, and foreign exchange earning sectors.

Socially, men must transform the old culture in ways which make it compatible with modern activities and institutions. The face-to-face relations and warm, powerful family ties of a traditional society must give way to more impersonal systems of evaluation in which men are judged by the way they perform specialized functions in the society. In their links to the nation, to their professional colleagues, to their political parties, men must find partial alternatives for the powerful, long-tested ties and symbols of the traditional life centered on family, clan, and region. And new hierarchies based on function must come to replace those rooted in landownership and tradition.

The small elite groups who dominate the political process in a traditional society are virtually certain to oppose change, for change inevitably means reduction in their status. When other elite groups capture power from them by either peaceful or violent means, the new leaders will be of many minds as to the evolution of their society. Some may seek to divert the national sentiment and the energies of the new national government into external adventure in hope of redressing old humiliations or exploiting newly perceived opportunities for national aggrandizement. Some may strive primarily to consolidate the power of the new central government as against contending regional authorities. Others may be interested primarily in seeing quickly installed the political and legal forms of modern democracy; and still others—initially usually a minority of the elite—may be anxious to get on with the concrete tasks of economic and technical modernization of the economy.

The confusions and cross purposes which result from this diffusion of objectives inevitably retard the process of modernization. Men may be tempted to seek escape from the frustrations of internal differences and to unite in aggressive attitudes or action toward the outside world. Or they may be led to accept in desperation the unity and discipline that Communist or other totalitarian forms of social organization hold out to them.

Although the small Westernized and literate elites play a disproportionately powerful role in the early stages of the modernization process, the mass of citizens must also be brought gradually into the main stream of change. Each person must begin to assume new functions and new relations to the economic and political process. The magnitude of the change required is suggested by the fact that the transition to modernization usually begins with more than 75 per cent of the population living in the countryside and less than 10 per cent literate. The round of life is tied to the rhythm of the harvests and to the narrow local scene; to a traditional system of land tenure and the assumption that life for the children and grandchildren is likely to be much as it is and has been in living memory. Social life is built around a close family; traditional political and social relations, long sanctioned by custom, tend to be passively accepted. The government is likely to seem a remote and distant entity associated with extraction of taxes and arbitrary recruitment of sons for military service; and the concept of the nation may often hardly exist.

All this must alter if modernization is to succeed. There must be a radical shift in balance to urban life, literacy must increase, agricultural methods must change, and the markets must widen and become increasingly commercial. Land tenure arrangements are likely to require alteration. The idea must spread that the physical environment can be understood and controlled in ways that permit higher standards of welfare. The government must come to be identified with activities and objectives that conform to popular interests. If democracy is eventually to emerge, the citizen must come to accept the responsibilities as well as the power to determine who shall rule and what the direction of public policy shall be.

By identifying the three principal areas in which the requirements for modernization may give rise to tensions and resistance, we have in effect defined social evolution in institutional terms. We have implied an approach to understanding the process of change in the underdeveloped countries based on characteristics which are given organized institutional expression in the social, economic, and political realms of life. But the more closely we examine our subject, the more evident it becomes that in the end we are talking not about institutions but people; that no division of the problem into parts permits escape from the fundamental proposition that the paramount requirement for the modernization of any society is that the people themselves must change. Our understanding of the process of modernization in the underdeveloped countries, and in turn our understanding of the policy problems involved, must be informed by awareness of the ferment of individual thoughts and emotions at the core of any drastic change in a society. Here, in what might be called the realm of psychological change, the requirements for modernization give rise to tensions and resistance, to visible and invisible conflicts which are often the hardest for the outside world to comprehend and accept.

To begin with, the instinctive Western feeling that all individuals, or at least all educated individuals, in a traditional society exposed to the impact of modern life should spontaneously value the goals of modernization simply runs counter to the facts of both human nature and history. It is of course true that virtually all individuals everywhere want some of the fruits of modernization—more income for themselves, more power, dignity, respect, and recognition for their countries. But man has ever been ambivalent and irrationally eclectic in his acceptance of the new, and hostile toward innovation when it violates long familiar customs and personal habits of thought. This holds for the member of a traditional society confronted by the demands made on him if he is to reap the benefits of modernization—even if he recognizes those benefits.

Thus to an individual who has absorbed with his mother's milk the attitude that it is wrong to speak or even think freely until the duly honored elders and persons in superior positions have expressed their opinions, the concept of freedom of thought and expression may be an impossible one to accept. He knows that in due time he will become an elder and be entitled to the deference of action, speech, and thought which youth owes to age and experience; and it may be unthinkable that this natural progression to seniority and deference should be abandoned in favor of individual equality of expression. One of the most pervasive carry-over effects of the traditional society is the persistent tendency to inhibit individual initiative, a perpetuation of attitudes that resist innovation in any form.

For centuries in the traditional societies it has been important to the more elevated classes to think of themselves as different by nature from the menial classes. Since one main mark of the menial classes is that they work with their hands and with tools, a man of higher status feels like a menial if he works with or even directs work with tools or machines. It is difficult for him to discard such inherited attitudes even if he is aware of them and tries to overcome them. His distaste for industry is heightened by the fact that the business and commercial groups in such societies (for example, the Chinese in Southeast Asia) are often groups who historically came from other countries and are still looked upon as outsiders.

At the same level of personal conduct, wherever life is economically precarious, as in traditional societies, it is common for all members of a group of relatives to share their income. The individual who gains extra income is obligated to share it with relatives who have less. Should he refuse to open opportunities for financial gain to his relatives because of what we in modern societies would term ethical obligations to his associates or to the public, he may be treated as a moral leper.

Thus the traditional guides to personal conduct become sources of inner conflict and resistance if the individual is to serve his society's needs for modernization. Even the educated man who sees the benefits of modern enterprises is deterred by custom from engaging in them because the practical problems of management are felt to be menial activities. Or, having accepted responsibility for a public enterprise, and understanding the modern criteria of skill and experience, he is still impelled by custom to use his position as a means of benefiting relatives and friends.

In short, the path to modernization opens up an almost limitless range of situations where the individual may be torn by the conflict of purpose in his mind and his emotions, a condition that creates obstacles to every aspect of social change. Such obstacles may be compounded by the high respect for traditional learning which marks many old societies; knowledge of ancient literature and philosophy is expected of every educated man, but study of the material world reflects menial interests and is thus sordid and uninteresting. Reverence for the ancient religion may be a further deterrent to change. One of the authors of this book remembers vividly the fear expressed by the fine old mother of a Burmese boy who had obtained a fellowship to study in the United States—the justifiable fear that in the midst of new experiences in the West he would lose his Buddhist piety. The case could be multiplied thousands, even millions, of times; it symbolizes the underlying loyalty to old values that makes modernization difficult.

The division of heart and purpose tends to be especially great in some ex-colonial societies, where the people as a whole may be diverted from constructive effort by emotions surviving from the past. The colonial administrators, by violating ancient family rights in land and other property, showing contempt for the indigenous religion, and treating the colonial people as an inferior race, may have intensified the ambivalence in the attitude of the indigenous population toward the West. The colonials respected the power of the Westerner and imitated his manner of living, but at the same time they often resented his presence, hated his behavior, and were determined to eject him and what he stood for, including his business enterprises. Now, after gaining their independence, such people may cling to the old all the more compulsively because to abandon it would be to admit that the colonial administration was right, that they were an inferior people.

We must, then, accept the fact that no matter how passionately in one part of their beings men may want to see their societies and themselves enjoy the benefits of modernization, they are capable of sustaining in tolerable psychological order only a limited rate of change; and they may cling more tenaciously than even they are aware to elements in the traditional society as a source of security in a transitional situation where almost everything else about them is changing. Even within the literate elite in the changing societies, who may be quite skilled and may talk the language of modernization with fluency and apparent conviction, there is often latent conflict between the modes of action and the values that modernization requires and the ingrained habits and attachments of the traditional society.

We must approach the problems of the underdeveloped societies with the realization that the modernization process requires fundamental human attitudes to change in such ways as to make the efficient operation of a modern society not only possible but also psychologically congenial. We must be aware that, especially in the first generations of the transition, the commitment of men to the goal of modernization may be more apparent than real.

Agricultural Innovations and Community Development

by STEPHEN ENKE

The rural village is still the center of life for over a billion inhabitants of the undeveloped world. These small villages, often comprising a hundred-odd people and a few extended families, are important units of the rural economy. If these people are to improve their lot, it will be through interacting schemes of agricultural and community development. But more than their own welfare is at stake. As we have seen, unless food supplies can be increased, industrialization will find itself checked. A rather stark program for agriculture is essential to any over-all plan of forced economic development. Whether this can be accomplished in a free society is not at all certain.

Role of Agriculture in Development

Agriculture and peasants are the twin rocks upon which all Communist and most "neutral" governments have almost foundered in their voyage toward industrialization and development. This is not because the Communist states have ignored and neglected agriculture; on the contrary, attempts to mechanize the cultivation of certain crops have been an outstanding feature of Soviet agricultural programs, and the Chinese have deliberately revolutionized the village communities for economic and political reasons.

Thus the attitude of non-Communist governments to agricultural innovation and community development is in sharp contrast. Their educated white collar officials tend to know little of village

SOURCE: Reprinted from Stephen Enke, *Economics for Development,* © 1963, by permission of Prentice-Hall, Inc., Englewood Cliffs, New Jersey.

life and seem to care less. As the Food and Agricultural Organization has stated:

The comparatively junior position which agriculture occupies . . . tends to be reflected in the low priority given within (member) governments to agricultural matters. Even when very large sums are being allocated to economic development schemes, the emphasis may be largely on the industrial side, and although the idea of achieving balanced development may be present in the minds of the planners, agriculture may in the end have insufficient funds for this to be achieved.[1]

The low status of agriculture in most undeveloped countries is also indicated by the disinterest of ambitious young officials. How to use manure and skin animals, for example, are not subjects likely to help them professionally. Some of these men are only a generation or so removed from village life themselves, and they wish to make good their escape by securing a government post in some provincial or national capital. It has been aptly remarked that "agriculture is regarded as an unprofitable and undesirable career, with little prestige value, small chance of promotion, and few of the other rewards that go to attract young men into public service."[2]

One of the important contributions that the Ford Foundation has made to Indian development is the example of interest and participation set by its senior mission officials in agriculture. That important and successful Americans and Britons should bother about the dirty and ordinary details of farming and village life is a constant source of surprise to minor bureaucrats, who are far too proud of their clean hands, white collars, and limited education. (The importance attributed to agriculture and conservation by imperial governments is also one of the offsetting and positive characteristics of recent colonialism.)

The widespread neglect of agriculture in poor and backward countries, however understandable it may be psychologically, makes no economic sense at all. Directly or indirectly, agriculture contributes about half the gross national product of many of these

---

[1] United Nations Food and Agricultural Organization, *Millions Still Go Hungry* (Rome, 1957), p. 6.
[2] Ibid.

countries when subsistence output is adequately valued and included. And economic planners, even if their only goal is industrialization, should realize two logical and associated requirements for agriculture and village life.

First . . . industrialization and urbanization require a greater total food availability. Most of this increment must usually come from domestic output. For centuries economists have agreed that more wage goods are a prerequisite of industrial expansion and urban growth.

Second, although the pace of industrialization may be established in part by capital accumulation rates, the industrial sector must receive its labor force from the original subsistence subeconomy. If agriculture becomes too productive, there will be a tendency for rural communities to withhold their labor from the rest of the economy. Only as the terms of trade shift against agriculture will labor tend to be released. This natural process of reallocation may be too slow for planners. In order to hasten the migration from country to town, they may wish to extract all increments of agricultural output from village communities, making these extra supplies available exclusively to city inhabitants.

Putting it bluntly, if planners wish to force the pace of industrialization and urbanization, they must arrange that (1) villages produce more food, (2) villagers have less to eat per capita, and (3) extra food is made available to urban families at what amounts to subsidized prices.

The Communist method has usually been to establish collective farms, conscript rural labor into them, and require these collectives to surrender or "sell" large output quotas to government for urban sale and distribution. Even if the Communists had no ideological need to terminate ownership of the land—private ownership of the means of production being counter to socialism—the exigencies of industrialization would have required some kind of food exactions by government. Unfortunately for the Soviets, their methods have not encouraged peasants to grow food for others' consumption, and it may be that economic growth would have been more rapid had the State placed less heavy a hand on agriculture.

Supposedly, democratic governments determined to force industrialization may have to use less obvious methods of extortion and coercion. They may be able to use the price system, if it is supplemented by taxes and subsidies, and if they will take the lead in sponsoring experimental innovations. Because they are not opposed to private ownership of the means of production, democratic nations may be able to make private land ownership an important incentive to medium-scale farmers. In this respect the non-Soviet countries have an important advantage—if they can learn how to use it. But so far, land "reform" has tended to fragment land use and reduce output, as explained in a following section.

City dwellers and most economists do not seem to realize the extent to which modern science is continuously revolutionizing agriculture in the advanced countries. In Great Britain, the agricultural revolution was as drastic as the Industrial Revolution, and the latter would have been impossible without the former. And it is still continuing. The ability of a little over 10 per cent of the United States labor force to produce agricultural goods for the entire American people, and to create surpluses for export besides, would never have been possible without new and better seeds, fertilizers, breeding, equipment, and widespread application of scientific methods. Can a similar revolution be expected among the primitive agriculturalists of today?

It is instructive to realize how these innovations have come to be made. In Great Britain, but far more so in the United States, the government has supported experimental stations to evolve and prove new strains of seed and livestock. Agricultural colleges have long been a landmark of nearly all the states. Many farmers have subscribed to technical farm periodicals, sent for pamphlets, listened to extension agents' lectures, and generally sought to improve their operations. In all this they have enjoyed many advantages. They are nearly all literate, and many have attended agricultural colleges or extension courses.

A substantial minority of farmers are well-to-do, have large holdings, and constitute good loan risks. Hence economies of scale—except in parts of the Old South in the United States—accrue to their farms and ranches. Moreover, where the operator owns his own land, apart from government regulations he is an independent decision-maker when it comes to land use, selection of crop, methods of cultivation, and so on. He does not have to make his operation conform with the practices of all his neighbors. Farming is not a community affair.

The situation is very different in most parts of the undeveloped world. Land is often owned and used by the subtribe, village, or extended family, and no important innovation in agriculture is possible without the agreement of the group. There is sometimes no way in which the community as a whole can borrow for equipment or improvements. Moreover, each family may cultivate its own paddy, or strip, or terrace. Where land is scarce, these individual plots may be small indeed. With small holdings, no single family can afford or justify the use of mechanical aids which are often commonplace in the Western world. Communal grazing makes it difficult or impossible to improve livestock by selective breeding. Peasant cultivators often know little more about agriculture than has been handed down as traditional wisdom from father to son. Few of them are really literate, most are superstitious, and there is a general resistance to outside ideas. When one realizes that a single crop failure can mean starvation, and that the advice of government officials has not always proved to be successful, one can understand the conservatism of villagers.

The first question therefore is whether today's villagers and primitive agriculturalists can significantly improve their operations within the present rural context. Or must small holdings be combined? Do current landlord-tenant relations have to be revised or abolished? Can agriculture be advanced without drastic alteration in the structure and organization of tens of millions of villages? Can anything be done within the existing rural framework?

Possibilities of Innovation Without Reorganization

At the outset, it is important to realize that many private innovations regarding domestic animals and crops *have* taken place, although sometimes this has taken a century or so of trial and error. Thus "Indian" corn (or maize), from which "mealies" are made throughout Africa, was introduced from the New World. Although sweet potatoes are indigenous to Peru, they are also grown throughout the tropics and subtropics. Manioc is another case in point. Cocoa was introduced into Ghana by small cultivators rather recently. Turkish tobacco originated in the Near East, but is now grown in parts of Asia, Latin America, and Africa as a cash crop by peasants with limited capital. Wheat and barley are today grown throughout the world, but they originated in Asia Minor. Long staple cotton has been transplanted from the Nile Valley to coastal Georgia and elsewhere. Chickens and goats are now commonplace in Latin America, but they were introduced by the Spanish and Portuguese. Brahmin bulls from India are being crossbred in the United States, Australia, and Africa. Eucalyptus or "gum trees," grown in many countries for posts, shade, and fuel, come from Australasia. The Israeli citrus fruit industry is not truly indigenous. The palm tree, useful for copra and much else besides, was imported into Oceania. Coffee and cane sugar are now grown around the world. Caribbean breadfruit was introduced from Tahiti. And the tree rubber industry of Malaya was founded upon seedlings smuggled from the Amazon Valley. Similar innovations are still continuing as private farmers and government agricultural stations experiment to discover what crops and animals can be made suitable for regions that have never known them before. A striking aspect of development is that one increasingly finds the same domesticated flora and fauna in all parts of the world where climate is similar.

Seemingly ignorant villagers have always made rather more innovations than is always realized. This is especially so where agricultural change requires little capital and is possible without wrenching the social structure. Dr. McKim Marriott's description of innovations in a small Ganges valley community could have been written of many other undeveloped villages:

I was very impressed by evidence of American influence—influences much older than those of Point IV. Farmers were cultivating potatoes, maize, tomatoes, and a strain of improved cotton, all of them imported from

America. I was surprised, too, to find many crops in the village which I knew were not native to the Ganges valley. Carrots, originally from Asia, were being eaten in huge quantities by men and beasts instead of the native turnip. Mustard oilseed plants were crowding wheat and barley in the grain fields; villagers told me that there had been none two generations ago. Sugar cane of an improved variety was being cultivated in my village as a valuable small cash crop, while it had become the only crop in other villages beside the canal a few miles away.[3]

But although some change is always occurring, the juxtaposition of new and old methods of village agriculture is often surprising, especially in Asia and Africa. The village flour mill may be powered by a gasoline engine, but the grain may be threshed by the hooves of circling oxen. Homemade seed-drills may be used instead of hand sowing, but reaping may be done with a short-armed hand sickle. The raising of water for irrigation, using traditional methods, may require several men, a span of oxen, and a week's work to water a single acre of land under cultivation.

The task of technical assistance to agriculture is therefore not to introduce change where there has been none. It is to ascertain what further innovations are practicable and worthwhile, given the numerous constraints imposed by the villagers' poverty, their other economic and social needs, and sometimes their overpopulation relative to land. The following examples give some idea of what can be done within the present context of village life.

1. It sometimes happens that, although a crop may have been grown in some area for thousands of years, scientific plant breeding for seed production can increase yields, reduce losses to local diseases, and provide a food of higher nutritional value. Thus, during the 1950's, improved strains of wheat and barley were developed for use in the Near East. Some twenty-five nurseries were established within the region, plus another ten outside, growing identical collections of wheat and barley varieties. Tests were made according to a uniform plan for resistance to bunt and rust. When improve-

[3] McKim Marriott, "Technological Change in Overdeveloped Rural Areas," *Economic Development and Cultural Change,* December, 1952.

ments can be made by outside technicians in seed strains of crops that have been planted in the same area for millennia, one realizes how great are the potential gains from introducing novel grains, vegetables, and fruits, and adapting them to local environments.

2. Many cash crops have to be processed close to where they are grown because of the inevitable waste of material and loss of weight. Examples are sugar cane crushing and sisal pulping. Many other plants—such as *cabuya*—require decorticating. Small holders who grow such crops for cash are usually faced with the choice of tediously transporting their bulky crops to the nearest mill, or inefficiently removing some of the wastes themselves. And yet, assuming that improved roads and transportation are often uneconomic, a little ingenuity, capital, and enterprise can often evolve an economical and movable machine for processing these crops. Compared to a large permanent mill, such devices must be very inefficient by physical standards, but portable decorticators have proved themselves in Costa Rica for *cabuya*, and experiments have been made elsewhere in pulping sisal and crushing sugar cane. Too often the problem now is not that the peasant can't grow a crop, bad though the soil and climate may be, but that he cannot make adequate use of what he has raised.

3. Fish are potentially an important source of animal protein, and an important fraction of the undeveloped world's villages are on a coastline. These people are accustomed to fishing, often using methods "perfected" thousands of years ago, but a night's work for a boatload of men may result in a very small catch. Often fishery experts, by suggesting the use of different lines and hooks, or different kinds of nets and methods of casting, can significantly increase the landed catch. Even the installation of a small motor in each fishing boat, so that further banks can be reached or a deeper drag can be made, may pay for itself within a season. Techniques of commercial fishing have been changing rapidly during the past fifty years in the Western world, but few governments of backward countries have taken steps to communicate these improvements to their own fishing villages, let alone make the necessary gear available for rent or sale or loan.

4. Leather from animal hides is an important material for making shoes, harness, belts, and the like. But the value and quality of leather is affected by the method of skinning, curing, and tanning. In countries where cattle are not slaughtered (for religious reasons), leather must be obtained from "fallen" animals, which must be found before vultures and hyenas spoil the hide. In India, the flayers or *chamars* are of low caste and little education. However, several experimental projects under technical assistance programs have resulted in increasing the number of skins recovered and improving the quality of tanned leather. Improvements in curing and tanning are probably also possible in other backward areas of the world. Moreover, as hides and leather can always be sold, there is an immediate cash incentive to making these changes.

5. Selective breeding and slaughter of domestic animals would increase food and protein availability in almost every undeveloped country. The situation in India, where 200 million starving cattle are competing for food and land with 400 million starving people, is altogether too familiar; were it not illegal to kill bovine animals, slaughtering three-quarters of the cattle population would probably double meat production permanently, significantly increase the availability of food grains to humans, and cereal shipments by the United States to India under P.L. 480 might be unnecessary. But quite apart from India, in many other countries male domestic animals are neither segregated nor sterilized, so that reproduction is indiscriminate. If livestock improvements in Europe and North America give any indication, meat production in many backward countries could be more than doubled through selective breeding and slaughter. Unfortunately, livestock ownership is often for status rather than food, and in parts of Africa cattle can be used to pay the bride price irrespective of their health or quality. A first and essential change is for backward peoples to consider livestock from an economic rather than a religious or social viewpoint.

6. Many areas of the world possess a comparative advantage in fruit and vegetable production, and could have a considerable domestic and export industry besides, if there were only adequate canning and preserving facilities. Foods that spoil very rapidly, such as

fish and milk, would often be produced in greater quantity if the practical market were not limited to the immediate village. But in hot countries, where transportation to the nearest town may be slow or uncertain, spoilage is too great a risk and cost. Government might make a major contribution in some localities by organizing low-investment and small-scale canneries that can be supervised by a single, skilled foreman. Probably the development of such plants is technically feasible and economically worthwhile. But small canneries are not a very dramatic form of industrialization unfortunately.

7. Increased use of fertilizers is often advocated by agricultural experts from advanced countries. But the use of manure is well understood in countries where there is population pressure, and Asiatic peasants have been known to walk a mile or more in order to defecate on their own land. In seriously overpopulated areas, few trees or bushes remain for fuel, and so animal dung must be burned for cooking. Dung that might be used for crops is also needed to plaster walls and harden floors of huts. If artificial fertilizers are not employed, it is often because of their cost, or their unsuitability to local soils, or the fear that when the rains come these relatively concentrated fertilizers will be washed away in the flood.

It must never be forgotten that in many poor countries, and especially those of ancient culture and excess population, the problem is in a sense one of overdevelopment. In the fertile areas that have water, every scrap of land is exploited, and even the roots of grass are used for nourishment. Marriott[4] mentions that improved wheat seed, advocated by government, was found most unsatisfactory by several Indian villages. Admittedly, with good weather the crop was doubled, but the grain from the new crop was so big and tough that the village women could hardly grind it in the old stone flour mills. Dough made from the new flour was difficult to knead and hard to bake into the usual consistency. The peasants didn't like the taste of the bread anyway. The cattle refused to eat the straw from the new strain of wheat. And the old straw was better for thatching roofs. All in all, the experiment was not a success, and

[4] Ibid., p. 428.

what seemed like a promising innovation failed because it was incompatible with traditional village life.

In a closely integrated village economy, no useful innovation is likely to be a casual matter. What appears as a simple improvement to a Westerner may have quite unexpected consequences. If this is true of the minor changes considered so far, none of which alter even land tenure and use for instance, the revolutionary nature of modern and specialized capitalist agriculture can perhaps be appreciated. Everything is so interacting that any "minor" change has wide repercussions.

Land Reforms and Agricultural Efficiency

A powerful countercurrent, running across the economic need for larger agricultural holdings, more trained supervision, and the use of equipment, is the almost universal political demand for what has loosely been called "land reform." There is land hunger everywhere. And "popular" governments, if beholden more to the masses than to any landlord class, have in many cases sought to satisfy this demand through ownership limitations and partial expropriation.

Some Degrees of Land Reform

Land reform can take many patterns, varying in degree of intervention by government, and is hardly a recent phenomenon. The French Revolution led to the end of feudal land tenure in Western Europe. Widespread agrarian reforms occurred in Eastern Europe following World War I. The occupation authorities in Japan after World War II tried to enforce maximum size holdings. Hope of land reform was an important stimulus to the Mexican revolution. And in Latin America and the Near East today, much of the potential revolutionary discontent among tenant cultivators is strengthened by the prospect of land seizure, these expectations often being sedulously spread by pro-Communists.

"Land reform" often means something less violent than revolution however. There are at least three degrees of government intervention that can be distinguished. The milder versions are usually to be found in countries with more established government and less uneven distribution of land ownership.

First, almost all governments during the past half-century or so have come to "codify" in statutes the old common law arrangements between landlords and tenants. These customary principles are often of long evolution, going back centuries in parts of Asia, while in Latin America many land tenure arrangements follow the pre-independence customs of Spain. The purpose of these laws has usually been to give the tenant at least the nominal protection of the courts against his more powerful landlord.

Thus the landlord by tradition may have had the right to evict a tenant for not fully working his holding, resulting perhaps from the death of a son and the failure of the tenant to hire a substitute; making such a provision statute law means practically that the landlord cannot simply give notice of eviction, but must convince a judge that the tenant is underworking the holding—and meanwhile the tenant is protected. Or the custom may be that a tenant is entitled on quitting to have the value of approved improvements he has made during the past five years; if this provision is legislated, the courts can be called upon to assess what is owed to the tenant, and this possibility may prevent landlords from capriciously evicting tenants who do improve their holding. Existing tenants often are granted "pre-emptive" rights by statute, the purchase price being a prescribed multiple of the least rental; provisions of this nature prevail in various of the Indian states, Uruguay, Japan, and other countries. By enacting land use and tenure statutes, governments have almost universally tried to improve the bargaining power of tenants versus landlords. Practically, though, this reform is too often limited by the inability of lowly and poor cultivators to afford the cost of advocates and litigation.

Second, governments have often tried to transfer income and wealth from landlords to tenants, typically by means of rent restrictions, limitations of maximum land ownership, and forced sales to small-scale cultivators. It may be required that to be enforceable rents must be approved by a local government agent. Landlords who own more than some maximum land area may be required to sell the excess on demand in parcels of prescribed size and at low prices established by public authority; to facilitate transfer of ownership, government may advance part of the purchase price to land purchasers as a low interest and long maturity loan, any subsequent price inflation giving the new "owners" a windfall. In other cases, large landowners have been given a certain number of years to disinvest themselves of all holdings above some maximum area, with the threat that land not so disposed will be confiscated by the State; the effect of course is that land prices are forced down to very low levels if the announced State policy is taken seriously, and if owners cannot divide their land among relatives. One form or other of these methods has been used to a limited extent by Pakistan, Egypt, and Mexico, and other countries besides.

Third, "revolutionary" governments in China, Cuba, and other countries have expropriated land from large owners, and divided their acreage into either individual peasant holdings or collective community farms. There will undoubtedly be other instances of such confiscation during the next decade in the Near East and in Latin America. A vital issue though is whether the new owners are to be individual families—in which case land ownership may eventually fragment or consolidate depending upon inheritance laws, population growth, and the advent of specialized farming—or whether "collectives" will be forced upon the peasants.

Politically, one of the most powerful propaganda weapons of the West against the Communist world is the desire of peasants everywhere to own land, not collectively as members of some government farm station providing food for the cities at low prices, but as private owner entrepreneurs. This is something the Communists cannot offer. But free countries must make sure that where land reform means extended peasant ownership, economic efficiency is not needlessly sacrificed.

Some Land Reforms and Their Economic Impact

Many of those who advocate land reform most stridently do so on supposedly humanitarian grounds. They observe poor cultivators in undeveloped countries, and these peasants are tenants, so it is concluded they would be better off if not tenants but owners. Or it is supposed that, because absentee landlordism and agricultural poverty are now associated, the end of the former would terminate the latter. The truth seems to be though that land reform, if supplemented by many other essential changes and improvements, is a necessary but *insufficient* condition of increased agricultural efficiency. Moreover, without these other reforms, drastic alterations in land ownership and tenure may actually reduce agricultural output per worker. Land reform and agricultural efficiency are not inexorably associated with one another. Hence, in a sense, it is dishonest to urge land reform as a means of increasing farm output unless plans are also advanced for ensuring larger holdings, investment of capital, specialization of output, innovation of crops and methods, and more aggressive entrepreneurship.

LAND RENTAL LIMITATIONS. In most rural areas of backward countries, rents are contracted in kind rather than money, and the landlord's claim is usually defined as some percentage of the output. Sometimes the divided output is net of replacement seed and stock necessary for next year's operations and some very minimal subsistence allotment for the cultivator. The landlord's share may be some traditional fraction, more or less unchanged for decades or more, but in the absence of legal restrictions this fraction is likely to increase as families and population increase in number.

The great merit of a sharing arrangement is that the tenant does not then bear all the risk of fluctuating output. Agriculture is notorious for dangers of loss from drought, flood, hail, disease, and pests, so that a poor tenant may seem perhaps to be the last person who should be called upon to assume all these hazards alone. This would be the case were he to pay a rent defined not as a share but as a fixed physical quantity.

The disadvantage of share rentals is that the tenant's incentive to produce is somewhat blunted. Extra output from capital improvements made by the tenant will accrue to the landlord in proportion to the rental share. Extra output from extra work enriches the landlord more, and fills the tenant's stomach less, than it would under some absolute rental arrangement.

34

All in all, if output rather than the tenant's income security is the test, land rental reform might usefully include the substitution of fixed rather than share rentals. By defining them in kind rather than money the tenant is at least accorded some protection against having to provide more output to his landlord in years of low product prices. Moreover, low city prices for food grains may be caused by good crops in other areas, which local cultivators did not enjoy in their region. 1380703

Most reformers are more interested however in seeing the average real level of tenant's rents reduced substantially by government *fiat*. The immediate outcome is without a doubt pleasant for the cultivator. He will eat better and can work less. Whether he will save more and invest these savings in agricultural improvements are another matter. Aggregate national capital accumulation will be less if the saving propensities of poor tenants are less than those of rich landlords. Another consideration is that, if land rents are kept artificially low by government, there will be more would-be tenants than available holdings. Potential tenants who cannot find tenancies will have to migrate to the cities or work as hired hands for those fortunate enough to be tenants when rent controls were introduced. The "shortage" of land holdings thus created will tend to freeze existing tenant-land relations. Where agriculture is undertaken for market rather than for subsistence, rental ceilings will prevent superior farmers from extending their cultivated acreage. Land rent controls can prove to be a very mixed blessing after their full effects have had time to prove themselves.

ENCOURAGING FARM IMPROVEMENTS. One common argument for land reform is that a tenant will be less inclined to make capital improvements to a holding that he does not own. Indeed, if he can find another farm later, he may deliberately overcrop and overstock and so exhaust the soil and grazing. As the Food and Agricultural Organization has stated:

The purpose of tenancy legislation is to establish equitable tenure relations which provide for continuous farming operations, sustained production, a reasonable standard of living for the cultivator, and his protection against undeserved eviction. Assured of the benefits derived from his additional efforts and from his permanent and semi-permanent investments the tenant will be encouraged to make all the improvements he possibly can and to develop the agricultural resources. Insecurity, on the other hand, and in particular, lack of adequate compensation for unexhausted improvements and disturbance of occupancy, will not only discourage initiative but may permanently damage the land by inviting soil-exhausting practices.[5]

The essential problem in any owner-tenant agricultural relation is to ensure that one or the other has an incentive to improve the holding and that neither has a motive for exhausting it. Where there is a comparative abundance of land, and tenants can move to other farms, economic policy should probably stress the protection of the landlord against malpractices by tenants. The usual situation is the opposite however. With the exception of certain areas in Latin America and Africa, most of the poorer regions of the world are characterized by acute land scarcity, in which case all economic bargaining power lies with the landlord class. But even here it is necessary to distinguish several situations. In some countries there may be many landowners, some of whom may not be much wealthier than their tenants, and in fact the same family over several generations may graduate from tenant farmers to cultivating owners to absentee landlords. However, this sort of mobility is not typical, except in relatively prosperous areas, and it is really more characteristic of agriculture in advanced nations. The usual situation in old and backward nations is that a few wealthy families own most of the usable land, that these absentee landlords live in the capital city or abroad and have no knowledge of agriculture, and that it is left to the tenant to make improvements and initiate changes.

It has often been stressed that tenants do not make significant investments and innovations in countries where land ownership is extremely unequal. But the usual inference that this is because the cultivators are tenants is not necessarily valid. In many of these same countries, as explained in the following subsection, the tenant now is protected against eviction without cause. He and his sons

[5] United Nations Food and Agricultural Organization, *Principles of Tenancy Legislation* (Rome, 1957), p. 52.

and grandsons are reasonably assured of farming the same holding, perhaps at a rental share that will not change, so that as a tenant he need not reasonably fear eviction from the land before improvements of his making have been fully depreciated.

However, it is still true that as a share tenant some fraction of extra output will go to the landlord, so that the rate of return to the tenant is less than the real output rate of return. An investment that earns 20 per cent for the economy, may earn only 12 per cent for the tenant, with the remaining 8 per cent going to the landlord. This must diminish tenants' incentives to improve the holding, and, usually being poor, their high time preferences already inhibit investment to some extent.

The ideal situation is where absentee owners, possibly through local farm agents, seek to improve the output from their lands through innovations and investment. Such enlightened self-interest might even cause owners to share in the expense of improvements in the same proportion that they share in output. Often landowners, or at least their agents, do suggest certain improvements and so are innovators in a sense. Best of all, some agents have been trained in agriculture at college, so that as paid employees of the landowners they become introducers of progress. In these ways large and wealthy landlords can often do more to improve agricultural practices than government can.

The pity is that only a few large owners of land seem interested in stimulating such improvements. Their daily social activities do not usually bring them close to their land or to their tenants. Often they do not feel any great need to increase their incomes, for taxes may not be really burdensome, and an ever-growing population increases their rents without effort to them. With thousands of tenants, no single landowner can bother about particular land leases, and his agents are normally promoted for their ability to collect rents and not for their proclivity to suggest capital expenditures. It is normally where an owner has a few tenants whom he knows, and lives in the countryside and gets around his own land, that unequal land ownership is associated with agricultural improvement.

Nevertheless, where tenants are secure in their holdings, one must not exaggerate the evils of having ownership concentrated among a few families who have no contact with their land. Under such circumstances, so far as the tenant is concerned, an absentee and renting landlord is little different from an absentee and taxing government to an owner cultivator. Thus some of the large land-owners of Latin America, whose ownership may derive from a royal land grant of centuries ago, still function really as tax collectors for the State. The owners collect rents from tenants and pay taxes on their land to government. The landlord's share of tenants' agricultural output has the same incidence as a proportionate income tax. And if crop sharing inhibits investment by occupiers, the true issue may be whether the rents that become government's taxes and landlords' consumption should not be defined absolutely instead of relatively, even if this does make the tenant cultivator suffer more during bad years.

The failure of peasants to invest may really be caused by factors other than their tenant status. So long as holdings are small, cultivators are limited in the kinds of innovations they can make, and practical objects of investment may require some extra work but few extra funds. It is not just that peasants are poor and so save little. The ability of agriculture to absorb capital improvements may be very limited within the existing social context and economic organization of village life. Schemes of irrigation and drainage require community agreement, and very often cooperation of neighboring villages too, so that there is little that an individual cultivator could do even if the project were not beyond his own strength. A single livestock owner cannot begin selective breeding where there is only communal grazing. And people who are poorly nourished, yet must work fairly long hours to feed their families and pay their rents or taxes, usually lack the physical vigor and spiritual energy to introduce major improvements. Impoverished peasant cultivators, whether tenants or owners of the land they work, cannot be counted upon for outstanding feats of agricultural enterprise. The real problem is how to reorganize village farming so that capital and entrepreneurship can be applied by government, landlords, or the community itself.

LEGAL PROTECTION OF TENANCY RIGHTS. In many countries the peasant cultivator, although legally a tenant, is protected in his holding and cannot be evicted without cause. Tenancy rights often accrue to heirs. Sometimes the owner can remove a tenant only in order to place his own son on the land. National laws often facilitate land purchase by the tenant, giving him the right to purchase at some preferential price, or perhaps allowing him to apply some of his rent to the purchase price. The object of such provisions is to help the peasant tenant climb the agricultural "ladder" to independent ownership. It is rather generally held that steady occupancy and eventual ownership should be within reach of thrifty and industrious cultivators and that these prospects are a strong incentive for him to increase his efforts.

Such legal provisions make most sense where agriculturalists can produce and earn enough above their immediate consumption needs to save the reduced purchase cost of the land they are cultivating. Where holdings are of reasonable size, where there is specialized production for commercial sale, and where perhaps farmer cooperatives and tenant associations enhance the peasants' influence and bargaining power, a substantial transfer of ownership may occur over several decades. Moreover, the tenants' savings that purchase the land may in turn be invested by the former owner in industry, so that this variety of land reform may channel rural savings into urban capital.

Unfortunately, there are many areas of the world where poor soil, unfavorable climate, fragmented holdings, lack of capital, and excessive population all combine to limit agricultural output and hence tenants' real incomes. In such situations tenants have no surplus to purchase land at anything like its real value. The very pressure of population that causes land to be cultivated intensively so that its rents increase, and which therefore elevates the capitalized value of its future income, prevents most tenants from saving enough to become landowners. The only price they can afford to pay is something a little greater than zero. And for government to compel sales at such a price would be confiscation.

Nor are there necessarily any economic gains to be had from

dividing the land among small peasant cultivators. The erstwhile tenant will certainly have no rent to pay, and so will live better, and for many reformers this is a sufficient end in itself. But output from the land may be no higher. The new owner may work less hard if all the output belongs to him and there are no easy ways to market the surplus he does not wish to consume. He will not invest in farm improvements if the holding is so small that he cannot employ most kinds of equipment profitably. This was well stated by one expert on Near East land use and tenure when she wrote:

. . . social change alone will not help, if there is no change in the methods of production: if the entire landlord class were abolished, while the methods of farming remained the same, bad years would still bring starvation to the cultivator and force him to borrow from one source, if not another.[6]

Where there is a large rural population relative to usable and available land, holdings tend to be small whether cultivated by tenants or peasant owners. The State can hardly make it easy for some favored peasants to acquire substantial land holdings if this means that the rest of the rural adult population must become a hired laborer class. When government seeks to satisfy land hunger, the results may be fragmented holdings, zero investment, and technological stagnation.

What Is Needed?

The basic economic inadequacies of land reform are well summarized in the following quotation:

In most land reform countries labor is cheap while land is the scarce factor of production. . . . In the economic development of these areas emphasis must be placed upon means of increasing both individual productivity and the productivity of land. One of the best means for attaining this end in agriculture calls for providing each farm operator with a unit of economic size and with the capital and training he needs to operate it. Unfortunately, this approach is often disregarded for the simple reason

[6] D. Warriner, *Land and Poverty in the Middle East* (London: Royal Institute of International Affairs, 1948), p. 121.

that there are far more people claiming land than there is land to go around. Too often land reform leaves the peasants with units of less than economic size or with units that permit subsistence but little margin for improvement. These units provide a poor base for the effective use of credit and for economic development in agriculture.[7]

The simple truth is that, unless supplemented by many other economic improvements, land reform of itself may accomplish little more than changes in the legal title to land. Otherwise, land reform does not normally result in increased output, and production may actually decline if the former landlords provided knowledge, supervision, capital, and perhaps marketing assistance. Giving land to peasants is not the answer. And even intelligent land reform tends to be a necessary but insufficient condition of agricultural improvement.

If agriculture is to contribute to economic development, both by producing more food and by supplying some of the labor and capital needed in industry, means must be evolved to introduce aggressive entrepreneurship. This is unlikely to come from the small-scale tenant, who lacks not only capital but also knowledge of what else he might plant and when. In some countries, where landlords are not too isolated from the land, incentive taxation may stimulate them to greater efforts. In other cases, government may have to abolish individual land holdings and vest local agricultural resources in the villages, appointing officials to supervise collective farm operations. In all cases, with means of transportation to market improving, agriculture must become more specialized. Extra value output must be sold to industrial workers. So-called "land reform" that does not introduce entrepreneurship to the village will be almost useless so far as economic development is concerned.

Modernizing Subsistence Agriculture

There will have to be drastic changes in village life if subsistence agriculture is to be "modernized." As suggested above, "moderniza-

[7] R. Barlowe, "Land Reform and Economic Development," *Journal of Farm Economics,* May, 1953, p. 185.

tion" includes at least the following: (1) combining land holdings, (2) specializing in output for market, and (3) introducing improved methods. These are now briefly outlined in turn.

Combining Land Holdings

Units of cultivation are often smaller than units of ownership. In countries where the peasants are poorest and the ratio of rural land to labor is lowest, individual family operations are usually too small to be efficient. Land fragmentation and parcellation, especially in countries where the law gives all immediate relatives equal inheritance rights, sometimes reaches such extremes that different branches of an olive tree may have different owners. A single family, instead of working a compact land parcel, may have strips of land in different fields several miles apart. And as population inexorably increases and more and more land is put under cultivation, the livestock have ever poorer land upon which to graze.

Simple arithmetic demonstrates that individual family operations cannot be enlarged unless other tenants or owners are forced off the land they are cultivating. Conceivably, where there are several families in a village that have more land and capital and ability than others, these families might be encouraged to "purchase" the rights in land of their neighbors. Government might acquire the land in the first place, indemnifying existing tenants and owners, and then lease compact land parcels to these "superior" and large-scale operators. The outcome would be something like the enclosure movement in Britain during the late eighteenth and early nineteenth centuries, except that it would be initiated presumably by government in selected villages, rather than at the request of influential local families. The dangers of such a program are considerable and obvious however. Corrupt government officials, responsible for determining whom to evict and what their land is worth, would have unparalleled opportunities to collect bribes from all parties. And only a very secure government could take the political risks of creating a large rural proletariat.

An alternative is to make existing villagers part owners, part cultivators, and part laborers, by "collectivizing" the useful land surrounding each village. The village then becomes an economic unit operating a single large farm. Existing owners (and perhaps tenants with inheritable rights) get some first claim on output, larger land owners presumably receiving less than proportionate liens on output. The rest of the village product, after subtractions for taxes and servicing capital borrowings, would be "sold." Some of this residual output would actually be marketed in town. But much of it would be paid as wages in accordance with the skills of laborers and the number of days worked.

The administrative problems and difficulties of "collectivization" are considerable of course. A supervisor would have to know the work contributions of each adult villager. Unless a strong *esprit* develops, villagers will be tempted to steal from the community's paddies and stocks, and to loose livestock they might still own upon communal grazing land. A perennial issue, especially if government extracts too much of the village output, would be the right of families to cultivate the land around their huts for themselves. In any event, there will be an unprecedented requirement for bookkeeping and supervision, lack of which will force government to experiment with only a few village "farms" at the outset.

Another burning issue would be treatment of underemployed living in each village. Is everyone to be put to work who asks for employment, in which case the worth of a daily work "ticket" at the end of the crop year may be small, reflecting a low marginal product of labor time. Or, if more labor is offered the village farm supervisor than he "needs," shall he take only what he wants; and, in this case, should he share the work and unemployment among the village's inhabitants by hiring them all a little, or should he fully employ a few workers, leaving it to them to share their earnings among relatives if they will. The answer is probably that labor should be accepted only so long as its marginal value product equals net urban wages, after deductions for special living costs in cities, and that hired hands should be as fully employed as possible so that others will be free to migrate to other jobs including those in industry. However, as the village farm supervisor who makes such decisions will be a government employee, politically these are all very difficult questions to settle.

Combining land holdings into larger units, even though the result is several large family operations rather than a single and integrated village farm, brings obvious benefits. One is that internal economies of scale can be realized through the use of more equipment and improvements, such as bore holes and reservoirs, power driven pumps, cattle dips, seed drillers and grain thrashers, and vehicles for transporting produce to market. Another gain from integrating land holdings is that a larger farm owner and operator can often borrow on easier terms. Still another advantage, explained in the next subsection, is that a larger unit can better afford to specialize in output. And such division of labor, partly because cultivators learn more about raising a particular good, is likely to increase productivity further.

Specializing in Output for Market

Land parcellation (or fragmentation) is both a cause and effect of mixed subsistence farming. If a family is to produce most of what is consumes, it needs perhaps some paddy for rice, some land for barley or wheat, some other piece of ground for root and fodder crops, another strip for sugar cane, and so on. Around a village, because of differences in soil and topography, certain land will be best suited for one use and other lands for alternative uses. Thus subsistence farming almost requires that each family have strips of several kinds of land. If each village family were to have a single compact land parcel, assuming that the land around every village is not uniform, such families would have to choose between less efficient subsistence farming or small-scale specialization. (Of course unless the size of holding can be increased, the latter may be inefficient also.) Land consolidation tends to encourage production for market because it discourages subsistence agriculture of mixed outputs that are too varied for efficient cultivation.

Specialization obviously incurs peculiar costs. Most of the output must be sold or exchanged for other produce, and selling and exchanging take time, especially if frequent and tedious trips have to be made to a market town some distance away. Unless these diseconomies are more than offset through enhanced productivity, specialization cannot be really advantageous, and it is exactly such problems of transportation that have encouraged the continuation of subsistence farming in many regions. This is undoubtedly one case where "social overhead capital," invested in railroads, highways, ferries, and the like, can contribute to the commercialization of agriculture. Output for market must evidently start in those areas from which towns are accessible.

Scale of operation and specialization for market are closely interacting. Without some minimum quantity of output to sell, taking goods to market is hardly worthwhile, especially where perishables cannot be stored and have to be sold upon ripening. Moreover, where a small-scale farmer has to carry his produce on his own head or on a donkey's back, a larger farm can perhaps afford to share the expenses of operating a truck.

Population pressure inhibits agricultural specialization for commercial sale. Where too many people are dependent for their livelihood upon not enough land, little remains for market after the family has satisfied its immediate needs, and there is really no reason to incur the additional trouble and cost of selling some goods to buy others. It is when families can produce more food than they can consume that the question of exchanging the surplus for nonfarm goods arises. And once it is realized that some of the output should be marketed anyway, the extra transport costs of output specialization are seen to be slight. Hence more productive farmers are more inclined to specialize, which in turn tends to make them more productive.

An important consequence of marketing agricultural output is that money is introduced increasingly into rural life. If the cultivator has cash for his output, he will pay wages and other debts in money, so that more people come to satisfy their demands through purchases. If a man has money to spend, he consumes what he wants, and not what he happens to have grown or raised. And the money that flows into a village from the sale of agricultural output eventually flows back to the town through the purchase of industrial goods. This means that both industrial and agricultural goods must be transported between village and city, and in opposite directions too, so that the cost of movement per item is reduced by eliminating "dead-heading."

Introducing Improved Methods

The greatest problem of all is to introduce improved agricultural practices into the villages. Part of this difficulty is that what constitutes better methods and crops is not always known with certainty. However, even when a desirable innovation is known to central government experts, it may require considerable investment. And even if no great capital requirement is involved, there is the difficulty of explaining and demonstrating the new method to villagers. Often they must also be persuaded that it is worth the risk of a trial.

Here it should be stressed that alleged "better" methods may actually prove to be worse. Many advanced practices in temperate zones are not necessarily advantageous under other climatic and cultural conditions. One example must suffice for now.

Superficially, the pointed nail plow that is common to so much of the Near East seems grossly inefficient, for it only penetrates a few inches into the ground. A modern molded board plow of Western design, which can invert a seven-inch sod in a continuous row, seems vastly more efficient. However, in hot countries with long dry seasons, deep plowing may cause a loss of moisture from the soil. Shallow groundbreaking with a nail plow may be good enough for the eradication of weeds that took root in the last wet period. Moreover, unless cultivators are willing to adopt contour plowing exclusively, deep plowing could increase soil erosion disastrously in some climates. Another problem is that a modern board plow requires a great deal of power, so that a pair of oxen might not have the strength to draw it, a motor tractor being required for the purpose. Not only do tractors cost money to buy and maintain, but fuel must be bought for them also, and their use is seasonal compared with oxen.

In most backward and tropical countries, a great deal of scientific research and experimental farming are needed to discover innovations that are biologically feasible and economically advantageous. Desirable methods vary considerably from region to region. Oil refineries of similar design using similar crude petroleum will have similar yields wherever located. But the same seed, although planted in the same way, may produce a very different crop in say the Orinoco Valley than in the Ohio Valley. This is so obvious when stated that it appears trite. The less evident corollary of course is that application of the same sort of experimental biology that caused the initial agricultural revolution in Western Europe, and which even in the last twenty-five years has more than doubled output per man for many crops in North America, is desperately needed in most poor and backward countries. Experimental agricultural stations, with trained staffs and adequate budgets, could be worth more than many spectacular industrial projects. New factories and machines are easy to see. But new knowledge of how a people can feed themselves better may be far more important in countries where a majority of the inhabitants are undernourished.

Once better agricultural methods have been proven to the satisfaction of agricultural experts, the problem remains of "selling" the new practices to ordinary peasants, many of whom do not wish to gamble a certain small crop against what they consider to be an uncertain though possibly larger one. At the outset, government may have to give new seed for planting, or it may have to guarantee free distribution of food grains should the experimental crop fail. Combining land holdings, especially where an entire village is consolidated into a single farm under government auspices, makes the introduction of new methods somewhat simpler. The village farm supervisor, probably hired by government anyway, can be instructed to institute certain crops and practices. Undoubtedly he will meet resistance, especially if no other village in the area has made the same experiment successfully, but free seed and fertilizers and guarantees against famine may assist in convincing the doubtful to make a trial.

Innovations always require some advance of funds or work. This is true even when purchases of equipment and materials with money are unimportant. The reason why "savings" are required is that any new method requires advance preparation, and this extra labor must be financed or fed ahead of output. Therefore accumulations of money or produce are needed.

Sometimes these advances may be considerable. For example, a new strain of rubber tree has been developed since World War II which yields several times as much latex as prewar trees did. Most of the rubber plantations in Malaya have been replanted with the new tree strain, but small holders have for the most part not made this change, largely because they lack capital. A new rubber tree does not yield for roughly five years after planting, and establishing new trees requires either clearing extra ground or destroying mature but old-type producing trees, so that initially the cost in capital of this eventually profitable innovation is considerable.

There are enough examples of plantation (or estate) agriculture in underdeveloped and tropical countries to suggest that modernization of agriculture involves not only consolidation of land holdings, and specialization of output for market, but also capitalization. Familiar instances are copra estates in Oceania, banana estates in Central America, cane sugar in the West Indies, coffee plantations in Kenya, and tea plantations in Ceylon. In all instances, scientific knowledge, strict labor supervision, and large capital sums have combined to produce exports, increase total employment, and earn investors a profit. The capital sector of a modern and developing economy should include agriculture as well as industry. And capitalist agriculture is as different from subsistence agriculture as chalk is from cheese.

In simple terms, development of backward economies is not exclusively a question of moving underemployed rural labor into industry and combining it with city-located plant and equipment. Another aspect of development is the moving of foreign and urban capital into agriculture and combining it there with rural labor. One advantage is that many of the associated and special living costs of town life are thereby avoided. Another gain is that increased agricultural output and lower food prices prevent unduly high urban wages and so render industrial exports more competitive abroad. Balanced economic development requires expansion of both a capitalist industrial and agricultural sector.

Over-all Community Development

The development of a village can hardly be considered complete when its agricultural activities have been "modernized" in the sense described above. The health and education of its inhabitants are still important needs. There is little object in having people eat more unless the incidence of gastroenteritis can also be reduced. If many of the village children will eventually work in industry, now is the time to give them the rudiments of an education so that they can manage later in an urban environment. Investment is out of balance when expensive equipment is used to clear and prepare land for planting but the village's water supply must still be carried from some distance away by its women.

Thus complete village development should normally include a safe water system, sanitary means of disposing of human wastes, and at least four to six years of schooling for children. These improvements all require labor, and a certain amount of material, and the supervision of someone who knows a little about civil engineering. Government may be able to provide the engineer during construction, and it may give or loan the village such materials as pipe, but the inhabitants will have to provide most of the labor and make some items—such as bricks—themselves.

Most of this labor will have to be "conscripted" in some fashion or other. The taxpaying capacity of most villages is not adequate to pay wages for community development. Government's police power can, however, be used in other ways to provide necessary labor.

One obvious possibility is for each local authority to impose a poll tax on all its villages, with the understanding that this can be paid in cash, in certain readily marketable food grains, or in labor for local public works. The rates of exchange between these three ways of meeting the tax would of course have to be stipulated. Then a man who had enough training to earn a good wage would pay in cash, and a man with a productive farm holding would pay in produce, while the comparatively underemployed and undertrained would pay with work.

The public projects financed in this way could include a water and sewage system, dams to prevent run-off during floods, a school house with classrooms for different grades, perhaps a local mill and smithy, paved streets in the main village, and a better road to town to facilitate transportation of produce to market. Such projects are well worth their cost to most villages. But they will never be undertaken without organization, some outside financial aid for materials that cannot be made locally, and enforced contributions of labor, produce, or money.

Complete village development in this sense can only be undertaken slowly at first. Even a country with a population of only ten million may have roughly fifty thousand villages. Few governments can simultaneously hire and deploy so many experts to initiate and supervise community projects, innovate agricultural improvements, and complete all the necessary bureaucratic forms. Moreover, until a decade or so of experience has been amassed, there can be no assurance as to what are the most productive improvements and innovations. So lack of personnel and expertise together require and ensure that over-all community development will proceed experimentally and selectively.

This necessity has other virtues however. It means that the first villages scheduled for agricultural innovations and community development can be chosen with an eye to cooperativeness of inhabitants, potential output increment, proximity to market, and so on. Government cannot afford to have its first model villages be anything less than successes, and so it had better select its experimental communities with care. Also, by locating model villages throughout the country, the demonstration effect will be increased. This should facilitate the indoctrination of other communities later.

The popular success that attends these community development programs of government will obviously depend considerably upon the amount of extra real income that villagers are allowed to retain.

If the cultivators are tenants of private landlords, the State can tax away much of the owners' economic rent while limiting the maximum rent liability of tenants. In this way the cooperation of the villagers—and also of course the political opposition of the landlords —should be ensured. If the State has consolidated village land holdings into a few large private farms, it can again tax economic rent more heavily, but this will hardly win for government the cooperation of what are now the most influential families in the local community. And if the State has instituted a single collective farm, increased exactions of produce will be bitterly criticized and become generally known elsewhere.

Most governments are anxious to force the pace of industrialization. And the tendency of most Communist governments has been to finance these industrial ambitions partly at the expense of agriculture. The "people's democracies" also afford a striking example of industrial growth that has been financed in part by forced collections and continued poverty for peasants. These examples suggest that taxation of the economic surplus realized by cultivators as a result of land redistribution, rent reductions, or other land reform programs can indirectly provide an important fraction of the resources needed for industry and associated urbanization. How large this fraction should be is largely determined in a free economy by commodity prices and prevailing rates of interest. How large it *can* be is something that only those versed in the art of politics and power can hope to discover.

3 The Economic Aspects

The central feature of modernization in most developing societies often appears to be economic change. This observation is true in that the more evident symptoms of modernization happen to be economic, such as the growth of cities and industry. There are, however, two far more fundamental reasons for the soundness of this proposition. First, economic development is a necessary requisite for satisfying a whole series of new aspirations and needs of people in a modernizing society—greater personal consumption of food, clothing, and housing. Another is the fact that economic change is one of the key factors causing the changes in values, motivations, and aspirations that we associate with the modernization process.

What is required for achieving a modern economy? W. W. Rostow has identified a period when self-sustaining growth begins, which he calls the "take-off stage." To attain this stage, the society must, it would seem, meet three basic preconditions: "the expansion of the society's human resources; the laying down of basic transport, communications, irrigation, and power facilities, commonly referred to as social overhead; and a radical transformation of the agricultural sector." In addition, each underdeveloped country should have a reasonably articulated monetary system, an active professional trading community, the core of a modern sector with some manufacturing activity already going forward, a moderately efficient system of government operation and administration with tax and fiscal powers, and at least a minimal communications network. The first selection below concerns itself with the immediate practical problems involved in the engineering of development. The second focuses on the need for industrial nations to revamp their trade policies in order to promote the economic development of the less developed countries.

The Engineering of Development

by ROBERT L. HEILBRONER

We must set ourselves two questions to answer. First, is economic development possible? That is, given the starting point, the deficient productivity, the lack of capital, the population pressures—in short, all the *economic* variables in the development equation—is it possible to arrive at a sanguine economic forecast for output and incomes in the developing nations?

And second, whether development is possible or not, how does a nation try to mount its economic offensive? What are the economic forces which can be brought to bear, what are the needed shifts in and additions to the collective national effort? In a word, how does a nation pull itself up by its bootstraps?

The Hidden Potential

From what we have learned about the strictly economic aspect of underdevelopment we know already what the core process of economic expansion must be. It must consist of raising the low level of productivity which in every underdeveloped area constitutes the immediate economic cause of poverty. This low level of productivity, as we have seen, is largely traceable to the pervasive lack of capital in a backward nation. Hence if such a nation is to grow—if it is to increase its output of food, to expand its scale and variety of manufacturing—clearly its first economic task is to build up capital. The meager productive capacities of bare hands and bent backs must be supplemented by the enormous leverage of machines, power, transport, industrial equipment of every kind.

SOURCE: "The Engineering of Development" from *The Great Ascent* by Robert L. Heilbroner. Copyright © 1963 by Robert L. Heilbroner. Reprinted with the permission of Harper & Row, Publishers.

But how does a backward nation begin to accumulate the capital it so desperately needs? The answer is no different for a backward nation than for an advanced one. In every society, capital comes into being by saving. This does not necessarily mean putting money in a bank. It means saving in the "real" sense of the word, as the economist uses it. It means that a society must refrain from using all of its current energies and materials to satisfy its current wants, no matter how urgent these may be. Saving is the act by which a society releases some portion of its labor and material resources from the tasks of providing for the present so that both can be applied to building for the future. Again, as the economist would put it, saving means the freeing of labor and resources from consumption-goods production so that they may be applied to capital-goods production.

This release of productive effort directed to present consumption wants, in order to make room for effort directed at the future, does not present an overwhelming problem to a rich nation. But the problem is different in a poverty-stricken one. How can a country which is starving restrict its current life-sustaining activities? How can a nation, 80 percent of which is scrabbling on the land to feed itself, redirect its energies to building dams and roads, ditches and houses, railroad embankments and factories, which, however indispensable for the future, cannot be eaten today? The peasant painfully tilling his infinitesimal plot may be the living symbol of backwardness, but at least he brings forth the roots and rice to keep himself alive. If he were to build capital—to work on a dam or to dig a canal—who would feed him? Who could spare the surplus when there is no surplus?

In capsule this is the basic problem which most underdeveloped lands face, and on the surface it seems a hopeless one. Yet when we look more deeply into it, we find that the situation is not quite so self-defeating as it seems. For a large number of the peasants who till the soil are not just feeding themselves. Rather, in so doing, they are also robbing their neighbors. In the majority of the under-developed areas, as we have seen, the crowding of peasants on the land has resulted in a diminution of agricultural productivity far below that of the advanced countries. In India, we will remember, a hectare of land produces only about one-third of the crop raised on a hectare in the United States. Hence the abundance of peasants working in the fields obscures the fact that *a smaller number of peasants, working the same fields, could raise a total output just as large—and maybe even larger.* One observer has written: "An experiment carried out near Cairo by the American College seems to suggest that the present output, or something closely approaching it, could be produced by about half the present rural population of Egypt."[1] Here is an extreme case, but it can be found to apply, to some degree, to nearly every underdeveloped land. It is widely estimated that between 15 and 30 percent of the agricultural population of most underdeveloped economies produce zero net output.[2] Whatever little crop they eke out is only won at the expense of someone else.

The Peasant Problem

Now we begin to see an answer to the dilemma of the under-developed societies. There does exist, in nearly all of these societies, a disguised and hidden surplus of labor which, if it were taken off the land, could be used to build capital. It is, to be sure, capital of a special and rather humble sort: capital characterized in the main by large projects which can be built by labor with very little equipment—roads, dams, railway embankments, simple types of buildings, irrigation ditches, sewers. However humble, these underpinnings of "social capital" are essential if a further structure of complex *industrial* capital—machines, materials-handling equipment, and the like—is to be securely anchored. Thus peasant labor released from uneconomic field work makes possible a crucially important first assault on the capital-shortage problem.

This does not mean, of course, that the rural population should be literally moved, en masse, to the cities where there is already a hideous lump of indigestible unemployment. It means, rather, that the inefficient scale of agriculture conceals a reservoir of both labor

---

[1] Charles Issawi, in Ragnar Nurkse, *Problems of Capital Formation in Underdeveloped Countries* (Oxford, Basil Blackwell, 1953), p. 35, footnote 2.
[2] Ibid., p. 35.

and the food to feed that labor. By reducing the number of tillers of the soil, a backward society can create a work force available to build roads and dams, while at the same time this transfer to capital building will not result in a diminution of agricultural output.[3]

This extraordinary feat of legerdemain lies at the heart of the economic side of development. It is not, however, just an *economic* feat. It is also intimately connected with another process which lies at the social core of development. This is land reform. For one cannot, after all, just go and "move people" in a living society. Deep-rooted legal and social institutions of landowning, of tenant-landlord and tenant-moneylender relationships must first be broken. Vested privileges in the old order must be overcome, often over the determined opposition of the landowning classes. Thus the mechanics of economic development immediately plunges us into the social and political problems of development.

But we can now also see something else of great importance. We can see that land reform is not just a matter of justice, of rescuing the peasant from the domination of a feudal landlord or a rapacious moneylender. It must also be a functional step, a step toward the formation of land units large enough to be farmed scientifically for high output. Land reform which merely breaks up large estates in order to parcel out tiny plots of soil is at best only a political palliative for the underdeveloped nation. Economically, it may even be a step backward toward fragmentation and inefficient subdivision.

However, let us revert to the immediate economic problem. We have seen how an underdeveloped society can increase its agricultural output and simultaneously "find" the labor resources it needs for development tasks. But where is the saving—the release of consumption goods—we talked about? This brings us to a second nec-

[3] In sparsely settled lands we cannot apply the same strategy because there is no surplus population on the farm. Here we must *create* a surplus farming population by first raising agricultural productivity through better seeds, better technology, etc. This "created" surplus labor force can then be set to work building capital. The basic concept of this great transfer of resources is elegantly set forth in Ragnar Nurkse's classic *Problems of Capital Formation in Underdeveloped Countries.*

essary step in our process of capital creation. When agricultural productivity has been enhanced by the creation of larger farms (or by improved techniques on existing farms), *part of the ensuing crop must be saved.*

In other words, whereas the peasant who remains on the soil will now be more productive, he cannot enjoy his enhanced productivity by eating up all his larger crop. Instead, the gain in individual output must be siphoned off the farm. The extra crop raised by the fortunate peasant must be saved by him, and shared with his formerly unproductive cousins, nephews, sons, and daughters who are now at work on capital-building projects.

We do not expect a hungry peasant to do this voluntarily. Rather, by taxation of various sorts, or by forced transfer, the government of an underdeveloped land must arrange for this essential redistribution of food.[4] *Thus in the early stages of a successful development program there is apt to be no visible rise in the peasant's food consumption, although there must be a rise in his food production.* Instead, what is apt to be visible is a more or less efficient, and sometimes harsh, mechanism for assuring that some portion of this newly added productivity is "saved"—that is, not consumed on the farm, but made available to support the capital-building worker. That is why we must be very careful in appraising a development program not to measure the success of the program by individual peasant living standards. For a long time, these may have to remain static—possibly until the new capital projects begin to pay off.

What we have just outlined is not, let us repeat, a formula for immediate action. In many underdeveloped lands, as we have seen, the countryside already crawls with unemployment, and to create a large and efficient farming operation overnight would create an intolerable social situation. Nor should we believe that the creation of such a modern agricultural sector can, in fact, be achieved overnight. Peasants, no matter how impoverished their condition, do not acquiesce gladly in radical rearrangements of traditional ways, nor

---

[4] Nurkse makes a sage comment in this regard. Speaking of the use of collective farms in Russia he writes: "The word 'collective' has here a double meaning. The collective farm is not only a form of collective organization; it is above all an *instrument of collection.*" Op. cit., p. 43 (italics added).

do they relinquish without protest their tiny properties or their traditional connection with the soil. In the communist countries the collectivization of peasant holdings has everywhere been bitterly opposed. In nations as different as Cuba, China, Poland, and Yugoslavia, zealous attempts to "reform" peasant attitudes and institutions have met with determined resistance, even to the point of sabotage. Nor have milder methods, such as the formation of cooperatives in India, met with much success in the face of inadequate educational backgrounds and technical experience.

Thus the social changes required to bring about a substantially improved condition of agriculture are likely to present severe problems to development-minded governments, authoritarian or democratic. Yet from the logic of the process there is no escape. In nearly every backward land, agricultural productivity *must* be enhanced if development is to take place, not alone to provide growing populations with food, but to create a labor supply for the formation of capital. Hence an amalgamation of small farming units into large ones, and a displacement of a considerable portion of the peasantry from the land, is a necessity for almost every developing country, no matter how painful the procedure.[5] The rate at which this can be accomplished, however, is apt to be slow. At best, we can envisage the process as a long-term transformation which extends over many years. It shows us, nonetheless, that a basic mechanism of development is the enforcement of a huge internal migration from agricultural pursuits, where labor is wasted, to industrial and other pursuits, where it can yield a net contribution to the nation's progress.

Industrialization

We have seen how a backward society has the hidden potential to build social capital. But capital-building is not just a matter of

[5] In the West, the absence of the extreme population pressure characteristic of the underdeveloped lands made this rationalization of agriculture a less pressing precondition of development. Nonetheless, a rationalization process took place in many parts of Europe, especially in Northern Germany and England. England's early economic impetus was much facilitated by the enclosures which, by the mid-nineteenth century, had transferred half the arable land from smallholders to large commercial estates.

freeing men and food. Peasant labor may construct roads, but it cannot with its bare hands build the trucks to run over them. It may throw up dams, but it cannot fashion the generators and power lines that are needed if a dam is to produce energy. In other words, what is required to engineer the Great Ascent is not just a pool of labor. It is also a vast array of *industrial* equipment, which is the integral core of growth for all modern economies.

Sooner or later every developing region, if it is to carry its material advancement beyond the level of a fairly efficient agricultural economy, must build such a structure of industrial equipment—a structure of machine tools and lathes, of specialized machinery of all sorts.[6] But there is a new difficulty here. For unlike the case of dams and irrigation ditches and basic housing, this new industrial capital itself requires prior capital. Roads and dams may be built, at least up to a point, by the sheer application of human labor working with the most primitive equipment. But lathes and looms, power shovels and machine shops cannot. The machines and equipment needed must themselves be made by machines and equipment. Thus there is a kind of endless circle here into which an underdeveloped country cannot break.

In fact, of course, it is not a circle but a spiral, for in the dim past the first machines were fashioned by primitive hand methods. If the underdeveloped countries had time, they could build an industrial capital sector much as the West originally did, by the slow process of accretion from handicraft. But time is what lacks above all in the race for development. Hence if industrial capital is to be added to the huge "public works" of social capital, the underdeveloped lands must find a way of bringing it into being in very rapid order.

What is that way? In part this critical equipment can be built within the developing country from its own manufacturing facilities, for only the most primitive regions have *no* machine shops or indus-

[6] This is not to say that every small nation-state of the moment, from Upper Volta to Viet Nam, can legitimately aspire to become a Switzerland or a West Germany. The point rather is that massive industrial centers must be built up within the great geographic regions of Asia, South America, and Africa if these entire areas are to escape from their present agricultural servitude.

trial capacity. But this is, at very best, only a small part of the total industrial equipment required. Many kinds of tools and apparatus are simply beyond the technical abilities of even the most advanced underdeveloped regions. And no underdeveloped country has even remotely the capacity to produce the over-all volume of industrial capital needed to sustain a rapid upward climb.

Hence the general answer to the problem cannot lie within the underdeveloped economies themselves. Instead, in the first stages of industrialization, before the nucleus of a machine-building sector has been laid down, the necessary germinal core of industrial capital must be obtained from abroad. Some may be purchased by the underdeveloped country in exchange for that part of its output which it has saved—i.e., not consumed—and shipped abroad as exports of raw materials or handicrafts. Some may be received as the result of private investment by Western corporations or individuals. And some may be had as "foreign aid"—that is, as gifts or loans from the advanced nations.

Thus for the first time we touch on the vital problem of the relationship of an underdeveloped nation to its more developed world neighbors, a matter to which we shall shortly return. But it is worth a moment's thought to place this relationship in proper perspective. Clearly, the pace of *industrialization* will depend heavily (although not exclusively) on capital goods obtained from abroad, whether by trade, investment, or aid. Yet it is also important to see that industrialization is itself only a stage in the over-all process of development. An industrial sector built before there is a supporting base of social capital, or before there has taken place a degree of agricultural reform, or before there has become visible some change in social attitudes, is likely to result only in an industrial enclave coexisting with a nondeveloped peasant society. Here are, in fact, the Damodar Valleys of India and the Union Minières of Katanga. For an industrial sector to take root, for it to exert a widespread economic and social influence throughout society, it will not suffice merely to bring in the machinery and equipment of industrialization. These must rather be planted in soil which has been at least partially prepared to receive them. Industrialization thus appears as the capstone of a successful development effort. And by the same token, the sheer growth of industrial output, without reference to agricultural output or to much less easily measurable skills and attitudes, is an inadequate index of the progress of the Great Ascent itself.

An Over-all View: The Take-off

Perhaps it is time to bring our investigations into focus. Hence let us assume, for the moment, that an underdeveloped economy has begun to change its agriculture, begun the slow metamorphosis of social habitudes, and succeeded in obtaining a flow of industrial capital from its own exports, from private investments, and from international aid. Can we then predict whether such a nation can commence a steady economic expansion which in time will bring it out of poverty and into the first stages of a modest well-being? Can we determine if it will generate capital at a fast enough rate to bring it, in W. W. Rostow's well-known phrase, to the point of "take-off" —that is, to the point at which its additions to capital make possible a *self-sustaining* increase in production?

An economist cannot answer this question for any particular country in the abstract. But he can isolate the main terms in the development formula which allow us to see how the different variables in the economic development process interact. They are three:

1. *The rate of investment which an underdeveloped nation can generate.*

   As we know, this depends on the proportion of its current effort which it can devote to capital-creating activity, at first largely of a social, later of an industrial, kind. Clearly, the higher the saving—provided, of course, that it goes into capital projects and is not merely hoarded—the more feasible does the "take-off" become. In addition, foreign aid, although not "generated" from within, can be counted as part of the investment of a developing nation.

61

2. *The productivity of the new capital.*

The saving which goes into new capital eventually results in higher output. But not all capital boosts output equally. A million-dollar steel mill, for example, may have a very different effect on output from a million-dollar housing project. We can see that the higher the productivity of capital, the sooner will take-off be possible. On the other hand, some "low pay-out" investment, such as schooling, is necessary in order to move ahead on "high pay-out" capital, such as a modern factory.

3. *Population growth.*

This is the negative factor in the equation. If growth is to become self-sustaining, the rise in output must proceed faster than the diluting effects of population expansion. Otherwise *per-capita* output may be static or falling, despite a seemingly large rate of growth.

Here is what might be called the "iron law" of economic growth.[7] So long as the amount of savings, coupled with the fruitfulness of that savings, result in a rise in output which is faster than the rise of population, cumulative economic growth will take place.[8] Each year an increment of output will be won over the year before, and this increment in turn will yield *its* increment in successive years. Even seemingly small annual gains can in this way pyramid in time to impressive amounts, just as a small sum left to compound at a low rate of interest will, over the years, grow to very large size.

On the other hand, if the amount of savings is so low, or the productivity of the capital projects in which it is invested so small, that increased output fails to match increased population, the result must be stagnation or even retrogression. And this absence of eco-

[7] The term is that of Dr. H. W. Singer.

[8] If, e.g., savings are 10 percent of income and if productivity ratios are one-third—that is, if each dollar of investment yields 33 cents of additional output—then over-all growth will take place at 3.3 percent a year (10 percent times one-third). As long as the rate of population increase is less than 3.3 percent a year, per-capita incomes will rise.

nomic growth will continue until one or more of the variables in the equation is changed—until savings rise, or the productivity of investment increases, or the rate of population expansion falls.

Thus economic theory begins to clarify for us the logistics of the Great Ascent—or, for that matter, of growth in an advanced nation. It shows us the principal economic variables which determine the great equation of economic progress. It allows us to think about a problem of enormous complexity within a fairly clear-cut framework of relationships. And to revert to the two questions with which we introduced our excursion into the theory of development, our analysis shows us not only that economic growth, starting from underdevelopment, is *possible*, but the mechanics by which it becomes possible.

Nonetheless caveats are called for. As we have been at some pains to indicate, development does not consist solely in, nor can it be solely measured by, quantitative output. At best a sheerly economic analysis of growth points to a necessary, but not a sufficient, condition of the Great Ascent; and in singling out the criterion of output, it tends to divert attention from the critical factors of social and political change.

In addition, an emphasis on the economic variables tends to make of growth itself a purely mechanical process. It assumes, rather than demonstrates, that such a thing as "sustained" growth in fact occurs once the magical point of "take-off" is reached on the development curve. Yet a number of economies—such as Argentina or Turkey—have "taken off," only to make forced landings; others—one thinks of France before the war—became airborne but never flew very high; still others, presumably in orbit, crashed—as did the United States in 1929. The variables, in other words, cannot be pushed to the critical threshold and then left to themselves; on the contrary, it may take nearly as much effort to keep growth going as to get it going.

Hence it is well to keep the iron law of economic growth in perspective. It is a useful tool of analysis, not a magic formula for success. But if we use it cautiously, it can help us appraise the chances for economic growth of the underdeveloped areas. . . .

Report of the United Nations Conference on Trade and Development

External Bottlenecks Obstructing Development

There is one dominant note in this report. On the international economic scene we are faced with new problems, new in kind, in some cases, and new because of the magnitude they have acquired, in others. We therefore need different attitudes from those prevailing in the past, and these attitudes should converge towards a new trade policy for economic development.

The problems that beset the developing countries are very grave indeed. They have to assimilate modern techniques swiftly in order to raise their levels of living. But new techniques, while they bring enormous advantages with them, are fraught with dangerous consequences, because we have not yet learnt fully to control the forces of development in a rational way.

The direct and indirect effects of technological progress are responsible for the fact that world demand for primary commodities is growing so slowly, to the detriment of the developing countries. The effects of the protectionism prevailing in the industrial countries are an added factor. Even though access to the markets of the latter countries is facilitated, the primary production of the developing countries should adjust to this slow tempo of demand, but structural difficulties prevent it from doing so to the extent necessary to prevent primary commodity prices from deteriorating in relation to those of manufactures. The further modern techniques permeate primary production, the stronger may be the tendency towards such a deterioration. Action by Governments is therefore imperative to deal with this paradox of development.

SOURCE: Reprinted from *Towards a New Trade Policy for Development,* Report by the Secretary-General of the United Nations Conference on Trade and Development, United Nations: New York, 1964, pp. 107–108, 112–125. (United Nations Publication, Sales No. 64.II.B. 4.)

Such action is also essential for rapid industrialization to become the dynamic factor in the development of the world periphery, just as primary exports were the dynamic factor in the development of the world periphery in former times. But in those days development had no social depth. Today it must. This makes the problem of development more complex and pressing.

The circumstances in which industrialization must proceed are, moreover, very adverse. The developing countries are still suffering the consequences of the disintegration of the world economy that followed upon the great calamity of the 1930's. They do not export industrial goods, except in very small quantities. Since their primary commodity exports are growing so slowly and their terms of trade tend to deteriorate, they lack the resources necessary to import, on an adequate scale, the goods required for a satisfactory rate of development.

These imports are mostly industrial goods, and only part of them have been or could be produced domestically on an economic basis owing to the smallness of national markets. They must export in order to enlarge these markets. But it is usually difficult to increase exports because costs are high, and costs are high because of the difficulty of realizing economies of scale in the absence of exports. Here too a policy is needed, action by Governments to break this vicious circle by providing reasonable access to the markets of the industrial countries for manufactures from the developing countries, and a decided effort to promote the exports of such manufactures.

The developing countries should also form their own groupings in order to plan and develop their industries in wider markets. In some cases they have only just embarked on this policy and they should be given firm international support in the technical and financial fields, within a more favourable institutional framework than now exists. Such co-operation is needed to help import substitution within the groupings with respect not only to goods but also to services, since maritime transport and insurance, for example, represent very substantial external payments.

Among the growing imports necessary for development, capital goods stand out prominently. Such imports have been financed in part by international financial resources. But, in addition to being inadequate, these resources present a further problem. The burden of servicing them grows heavier and heavier, and in some cases the situation is becoming very critical, again because the exports which must provide the necessary funds for servicing are expanding very slowly and losing their purchasing power, while the demand for imports continues to grow.

All these factors that are so unfavourable to the developing countries converge in the persistent trend towards external imbalance that stifles economic development. As was seen at the beginning of this report, it has been estimated that the potential trade gap in goods and services will amount to some $20 billion by the last year of this decade if the present course of events continues unchecked. This is a staggering figure from the standpoint of the developing countries, but not from that of the industrial countries, since the amount by which the former would have to increase their exports of primary commodities and manufactures in order to bridge this gap, to the extent that it is not covered by international financial resources, represents only an insignificant fraction of the latter's consumption.

The problem must therefore be cut down to its proper size. The remarkable development of the industrial countries has given them a high foreign trade potential. Everything depends on ensuring that part of this potential is translated into practical measures that would bring about a significant increase in imports from the developing countries.

. . . . .

The Responsibility of the Developing Countries

While technological progress in the industrial centres and its gradual spread to the rest of the world creates new problems at the international level, as was stated at the beginning of this part of the report, it also creates problems in the developing countries and requires new attitudes and gigantic efforts by the latter countries to solve such problems.

66

The obstacles in the way of this effort are formidable. In many developing countries, however, attention is often centred on the external obstacles; the problems seem more urgent there, perhaps because they are more conspicuous. But it would be dangerous self-deception to imagine that, once these external obstacles are overcome, the way will be wide open for spontaneous economic development.

On the contrary, the determination to overcome these obstacles and exert a conscious and deliberate influence on the forces of economic and social development is also essential. The policy of international co-operation is only complementary; it cannot be a substitute for internal development policy. Nor can the internal policy fulfil its aims without effective and timely international co-operation.

This report would therefore be incomplete if we failed to remember the nature of the main obstacles to be overcome internally. In every country there is a different complex of problems, and the attitudes toward them are also different; the risks implicit in these generalizations should therefore be borne in mind.

The Internal Changes Required by Development

Generally speaking, there are three main obstacles in the way of propagating technological advances and which therefore obstruct the growth of productivity and per capita income in the developing countries: land tenure; limited social mobility and the ignorance of the masses; and the concentration of income in the hands of relatively small population groups.

The forms of land tenure generally to be found in the developing countries are plainly incompatible with technological progress. This is particularly so, when a large part of the productive land is concentrated in the hands of a few, while a very large number of small and medium-sized holdings generally make up a tiny proportion of the cultivable land. All this conspires to frustrate development; in some cases, because the high rent already received by the landowner makes him reluctant to take the trouble of introducing modern techniques, and, in others, because the very size of the holdings and

the shortage of resources for investment are often such that contemporary techniques cannot be fully and properly used.

The ignorance of the masses and limited social mobility are two
aspects of the same problem. If up-to-date techniques are to penetrate, there must be opportunities for learning and training and easy
access to such opportunities. Conditions must also be favourable for
the most able and dynamic people at all social levels to come forward and get ahead. Generally speaking, this happens to a very
limited extent only, which means that a vast human potential is
wasted, just as the outdated forms of land tenure impede exploitation of the enormous productive potential of the land.

The concentration of income is, of course, linked to these other
two features and, in many cases, is aggravated by the serious effects
of inflation, a phenomenon usually also influenced by structural
factors. It might be thought that this concentration would actively
contribute to capital formation, but this is so only in exceptional
cases. More commonly, high incomes mean superfluous and excessive
consumption by the groups that have them, to the detriment of the
investment that technological progress requires on an ever-growing
scale.

It would be a serious mistake, however, to imagine that the
problem of capital formation could be fundamentally solved in most
developing countries, if this savings potential of the high-income
groups could be used for investment rather than consumption, and
if, at the same time, the flight of capital, which reaches rather significant figures in several developing countries, could be avoided.
There is no doubt that all this must be done and that the tax instrument should be used together with other measures for the purpose.
But in many countries the problem of capital formation has also to
be tackled resolutely with international financial resources, which,
by stimulating the rapid growth of income, help to create opportunities for domestic capital formation that are now extremely
slight.

The weakness of the development impetus in many of the peripheral countries is a result of all these internal factors that combine
in a particular social structure, in addition to the external factors

that hamper growth. Development calls for changes in the forms of production and in the economic structure which cannot come about unless a change in the social structure leaves the way open to the forces of technological progress.

Without such changes industrialization cannot run its full course. Generally speaking, industrialization has simply superimposed itself on the existing state of affairs without basically altering it. Furthermore, the excessive protectionism frequently sheltering industries adds a further privilege to those already existing in the distribution of income.

Again, industrial development is constricted not only by the lack of exports but also by the smallness of the internal market. Rural masses working generally in a very unproductive way, urban masses who, to a large extent, take refuge in very low-paid artisan occupations and personal services, or who waste their efforts in antiquated forms of trading—these do not provide a large and lively market for the products of industrial development. And industry itself does not generate, to the extent desired, the income that could create its own strong market; for excessive protectionism and restrictions on imports usually shield it from healthy competition and weaken the incentive to raise productivity and the incomes of the people who work in it through the efficient use of men and machines.

Industrialization and Demographic Growth

But the problem is not a simple one. The development of the domestic market through technological improvements in agriculture, better marketing organization, the gradual elimination of artisan occupations, and a gradual decrease in the number of people precariously employed in personal services, will release an enormous potential of workers who will swell the ranks of those who, owing to the high rate of population growth, have to be incorporated in the economy each year. It is the extremely important dynamic function of industry and other activities which thrive with it to absorb this human potential at a satisfactory level of productivity. If they are to fulfil this absorptive function effectively, all these activities must forge ahead all the faster as modern techniques penetrate to those strata of the population which are technologically so conspicuously backward.

The nature of this question should be stressed here, for it is still asserted sometimes that the solution of the development problem is to be sought in the domestic market and not in the expansion of exports.

The fact is that the development of the domestic market and the promotion of exports are not two alternative or mutually exclusive propositions. The two processes must take place simultaneously and in a co-ordinated manner. The penetration of modern techniques to the submerged strata of the population is an inevitable prerequisite for accelerating growth. If this acceleration is to be achieved, the persistent trend towards external imbalance must be overcome through the expansion of exports and other measures of international economic co-operation.

This dynamic role of industry and other activities in the absorption of the human potential is a key element in the process of development. In most cases, this role is not being played well. For example, in Latin America the minimum rate of per capita income growth of 2.5 per cent a year, laid down as a target in the Punta del Este Charter, would not be sufficient to bring about this absorption under the present conditions in which modern techniques are penetrating rather slowly. If the penetration could be speeded up, it would become even more imperative to expedite growth and industrialization.

Naturally, when the subject of accelerating development is broached, the question is often asked whether the developing countries could not themselves attain this objective by lowering their rates of demographic growth.

There would seem, however, to be very little prospect of achieving such a reduction in the next decade. Historically, the decline in the birth rate has been a consequence of industrialization and of improvement in the level of living, and this process has been very gradual. On the other hand, it is difficult to envisage the possibility of bringing about a sharp reduction in the birth rate quickly by a conscious and deliberate policy. It has been pointed out more than once that, even where religious considerations do not affect the implementation of such a policy, it would encounter formidable social, educational and economic difficulties. The success that might be achieved is therefore very uncertain. Actually, with the leeway which the developing countries still have to make up in order to reduce their death rates, and with persons of marriageable age forming an increasing proportion of their populations, the rate of demographic growth appears more likely to rise than to fall in the immediate future.

Be that as it may, reducing the rate of population growth cannot in any sense be an alternative to the vigorous development policy advocated in this report. It could not be a method of evading or slackening the effort which this policy necessarily entails; on the contrary, it would be a means of deriving more far-reaching and effective results from such a policy.

Development Planning and International Co-operation

All these considerations give us some idea of the nature and complexity of the changes which development demands. Furthermore, these changes call for a great effort to mobilize resources which, like the changes themselves, need to be given a definite direction and clear economic and social objectives. Hence the need for development planning.

Planning is something more than a new technique superimposed on the framework of public administration, which is usually so defective in the developing countries. Here again, basic changes are required both in thinking and in action, and such changes are far from easy to make.

Among the major obstacles in the way of planning mention must be made of those of an external nature. Persistent fluctuations and the trend of the terms of trade to worsen, added to the slow growth of exports, have been very adverse factors hindering regular economic development and hence the task of planning. It is very difficult to plan, set targets and quantify resources when the effectiveness of such action largely depends on external factors beyond a country's control.

If the whole situation could be corrected in a reasonable manner by means of an enlightened policy of international co-operation, the peripheral countries would be better able to fulfil their responsibility in the dynamics of development. This responsibility, far from decreasing, would then be greater than ever, for, if external conditions took a favourable turn, there would be no justification for any slackening or hesitation in the internal effort to expedite development.

All this calls for major political decisions, but these decisions cannot come from outside. Nor can agrarian and educational reform, tax reform, and, in short, the various measures aimed at effecting structural changes, be a matter for international negotiation as a counterpart of financial co-operation. They must spring from each country's deepest conviction and from its genuine determination to bring about such changes. What is needed from the outside world, however, is a large measure of understanding and support.

That is certainly not the meaning of those not infrequent admonitions to put one's house in order so that development can come about spontaneously. Maybe they are a remembrance of bygone days. In those days putting one's house in order was enough, given the resultant influx of foreign private capital and the expansion of exports, to enable the peripheral countries effectively to fulfil their function as producers of foodstuffs and raw materials for the industrial centres.

Today the phenomenon of development is very different and its requirements are usually not compatible with that order of things. It is true that one's house must be put in order, but in a different order from that sometimes visualized in these admonitory attitudes. These attitudes cannot be allowed to guide the policy of international co-operation. This policy must be imbued with the same deep sense of renovation as the internal policy of economic and social development, since it is its indispensable complement.

In all of this there is a clear convergence of responsibilities, internally as well as internationally. The controversy about whether internal ills are caused by external factors or whether the source of these ills should be sought exclusively in the behaviour of the country concerned has been rendered obsolete by events and is meaningless now. There are both internal and external factors to be attacked simultaneously. To emphasize the former and exclude the latter, or *vice versa,* would be an aimless exercise and only divert our attention from the real solutions.

The Concerting of Trade Measures

These solutions cannot be adopted in isolation, since they form an integral part of a more comprehensive policy of international cooperation for economic development. [These solutions are:]

Import Targets

With regard to primary commodities and industrial goods produced by the developing countries, it is advocated that *quantitative targets* should be set for their entry into the industrial countries' markets, to be reached within a certain number of years.

The import targets for *primary commodities* could be, depending on the individual case, quantities of specific commodities or groups of commodities, or desired proportions of the consumption, or of the increase in consumption, of each importing country.

The targets for *industrial goods* could be expressed for each importing country in terms of a *global value* covering the quota of imports of manufactures enjoying preferences and the minimum target of imports not subject to preferences that should be attained in order to help eliminate the trade gap.

Cases of *injury to domestic producers* resulting from exceptional increases in imports from developing countries should be dealt with under the normal procedures laid down by GATT.

Industrial Preferences

Within the aforesaid global value, the industrial countries could establish a quota for admitting manufactured goods from the developing countries *free of duty,* but they could *exclude from these preferences* a schedule of items constituting a reasonable percentage of the total goods they import. This exclusion could take effect from the outset or during the operation of the system, in accordance with criteria to be laid down.

Manufactures from developing countries thus excluded from the scope of preferences would be admitted by the industrial countries on the usual most-favoured-nation basis.

All the developing countries, irrespective of their level of development, would be eligible to avail themselves of the *preferential system* up to the amount of the relevant quota. But there would have to be a periodic review of the flow of exports; and if exports from one or more countries increased so much that they did not leave sufficient room for those from the others, equitable solutions should be sought.

Special preferences could be granted to the less advanced developing countries. For this purpose, the list of items excluded by the industrial countries from the preferential system applied to all developing countries should be used.

The preference would *remain in force for ten years* from the time when each industry in a given country started to export. But this period could be extended in accordance with internationally agreed procedures, if an *exception to the rule* was fully justified.

Existing Preferences

The ultimate objective should be to adapt existing preferential arrangements to the new system of preferences in such a way that there is *no discrimination among developing countries,* and so that developing countries presently obtaining such preferences should continue receiving *benefits* under the new system at least *equivalent* to those they now enjoy. The precise way in which this ultimate objective might be secured is a matter for further discussion but it should include, in particular, international technical and financial assistance to countries at the earliest stage of economic development.

In any case, preferences granted by developing to industrial countries should cease.

Nature of the Targets

The targets are an expression of the *objectives to be reached;* thus they are of an indicative character and, generally speaking, do not constitute commitments to import. But the targets for primary commodities, in addition to representing quotas of goods to be imported without restrictions, might constitute *commitments to purchase* over a number of years.

When the targets are set, Governments would pledge to take all necessary action to reach them, including *promotional measures in the technical, trade and financial fields.*

In the socialist countries, the targets would also be of an *indicative character,* but they should be translated into long-term commitments to import under the system of bilateral agreements.

Commodity Agreements

Two converging kinds of measures are envisaged to *guarantee the purchasing power of exports* of primary commodities: commodity agreements and compensatory financing.

Commodity agreements can be used to establish minimum prices or improve prices, as the case may be, by maintaining their parity with those of manufactures, when the price improvement does not *substantially affect* consumption by reducing it or by giving synthetics and substitutes a competitive advantage.

Commodity agreements should establish whatever system of *export quotas* may be necessary to support the price policy.

When internal prices are higher in the industrial countries than on the international market, the adverse effects on consumption could be avoided if the raising of prices was accompanied by an *equivalent lowering of tariffs or internal taxes* where such exist.

In the case of *tropical commodities,* the internal taxes should be lowered still more until they are completely eliminated, so as to encourage consumption.

As regards competition from *synthetics and substitutes,* there might be cases in which it is advisable to *increase productivity and lower the costs and prices* of some natural commodities, provided that the loss of income thus suffered by the exporting countries is offset through compensatory financing.

Whenever the temporary shortage of a primary commodity leads to price rises that adversely affect producers and consumers, *ceiling prices* should be set. The agreements should also lay down rules for the disposal of surpluses and non-commercial stocks.

The scope of commodity agreements, or of corresponding inter-governmental action, should be considerably extended and conditions should be laid down for access to the markets of the industrial countries through *import quotas* and *import commitments*, where feasible; in addition, provision should be made for the gradual lowering of *support prices* and arrangements made for co-ordinating the internal and external production policy of the importing and exporting countries. The purpose of all these steps is to ensure that the latter obtain a reasonable share in the growth of consumption of the former.

Compensatory Financing

Compensatory financing is imperative to the extent that it may not be possible, through commodity agreements, to prevent the exporting countries from suffering losses owing to deterioration in the terms of trade.

Two kinds of losses would have to be compensated *henceforth:* those due to *the previous deterioration in the terms of trade* and those resulting from *future deteriorations*.

The *amount of compensation* to be received by each exporting country would be determined after consideration of the effect that the deterioration has had on its investment resources and balance of payments, so that the country can receive whatever additional resources it needs to continue *its economic development plan* without disturbances.

These *additional resources* should not be transferred directly to producers, except where this is essential to ensure the normal development of production.

Each country should take whatever internal action it sees fit to obtain resources for *compensatory financing*. But it should not do so through taxes which, by raising prices for the consumer, *discourage consumption or encourage the replacement* of a natural commodity by substitutes or synthetics.

The compensatory resources might form part of a fund administered by *international credit institutions,* at either the international or the regional level, in accordance with rules approved by Governments.

The required resources might also be made available to developing countries by national and international agencies acting through consortia or by other suitable co-operative arrangements.

In either case, the relevant decisions might be based on an independent finding by an *international team of independent experts* of the highest standing that a particular country's economic development was being prejudiced by terms-of-trade losses.

Readjustment of the External Debt

Consideration should be given to the *readjustment of repayment periods* and terms of the *external debt* of some countries. External financing could facilitate this operation. Steps should also be taken to avoid the subsequent recurrence of critical situations resulting from excessive increases in the burden of servicing.

Maritime Transport and Insurance

The possibility should be examined of developing merchant marines and insurance operations within regional groupings of developing countries or of promoting among them specialization in the miscellaneous activities that constitute these services.

The system of shipping conferences and the impact of their agreements on the developing countries should also be examined.

Groupings of Developing Countries

The developing countries should pursue their industrialization policies and especially their *import substitution* policies and should endeavour to pool their efforts rationally by means of preferential groupings on as large a scale as possible.

These preferential groupings should be supplemented by *payments agreements* between their constituent members.

The GATT Rules

The GATT rules now in force should be amended to take into account the consequences of the structural inequalities between industrial and developing countries. These amendments should relate in particular to reciprocity with a view to establishing the concept of *implicit reciprocity;* to the *preferences* granted by the industrial countries to the *developing countries;* and to the *preferences granted by developing countries to each other* through groupings of countries.

Reduction of Excessive Tariffs

Without being committed to reciprocity, developing countries with excessive protectionism should undertake *to lower their high tariffs* as they gradually counter the trend towards external imbalance by expanding their exports of primary and industrial products and by import substitution.

Differences between the Developing Countries

In the application of these concerted measures, it is essential to recognize the different situations of the developing countries, depending on the degree of their development, and to adapt and coordinate the measures adopted so that the advantages deriving therefrom accrue in particular to the *less advanced of the developing countries* in order to give strong impetus to their growth. In this connexion, not only might the less advanced countries to be given general preferences, shared with the other developing countries irrespective of their degree of development, and special preferences, but they should also receive particular attention so far as the measures for promoting their exports are concerned. They should also be given special attention as regards the allocation of international financial resources; the per capita volume of the resources that these countries obtain should generally be greater than that granted to the more advanced of the developing countries and especially to those of them which may already have improved their ability to generate their own investment resources.

Nature and Adaptability of the Policy of International Co-operation

Now that the principal measures proposed in this report have been thus summarized, two important observations should be made.

The first concerns the very nature of the policy which embraces all these measures. It is not simply a matter of lowering or removing barriers which stand in the way of the developing countries' trade and of laying down more appropriate rules than those now in force. What is required is positive action.

This is the significance of the import targets. They are the tangible and practical expression of the responsibility which Governments—both of the industrial and of the developing countries—may decide to assume in order to achieve certain basic foreign trade objectives. And this responsibility would necessarily involve the adoption of whatever measures may be called for, both internal and international.

Thus, should the import targets set be insufficiently high, or prove to be so in practice, the inflow of international finance would have to be increased to cover the trade gap.

This does not mean that import targets and external financial aid are interchangeable concepts. Actually, the quantity of external finance should rather be a supplement to internal investment resources, to compensate for their present scarcity. Under normal circumstances, their direct role should not be to bridge the gap. This has to be done through the expansion of exports. Hence there is no conflict between trade and aid. Each of these has its specific role to play.

Consequently, the extent to which exports and international financial resources have to be co-ordinated is not arbitrary. The proportion of these resources in each country's investment programme

79

must become smaller in the course of time as domestic savings capacity draws strength from the economic development process itself. Exports, on the other hand, must expand continuously in order to cover mounting import requirements and pay for servicing the external debt.

All this points to desirability of periodically examining the way in which those objectives are being achieved, not as ends in themselves but as means which, in combination with others, would make it possible to reach a bigger target, the growth target set for the United Nations Development Decade and the more satisfactory targets which may be established later.

The second observation concerns the flexibility with which this policy must be carried out. The developing countries have certain very important common denominators, but there are also great disparities between them, deriving from their different degrees of development and from the particular problems that affect them. Owing to these disparities, the measures advocated here would also have very different effects from country to country. Thus, while access to the manufactured goods markets of the industrial countries is important for all, some developing countries would be able to enjoy the advantages of these measures much earlier than others, unless these opportunities are accompanied by very energetic promotional measures in the countries which would otherwise lag behind. Commodity agreements or compensatory financing would also have a very diverse impact. All of the foregoing emphasizes the need to bear in mind these disparities in degrees of development and in individual situations. The decisive element here could be international technical and financial aid. The intensity of this aid would have to be geared to those disparities so that all the countries could expedite their pace of growth, or maintain it in the few cases where an acceptable tempo has been attained.

This very heterogeneity opens up interesting vistas so far as the dynamics of development is concerned. At one extreme are the countries which are close to a level of income that will enable them, in a relatively short time, to grow at a satisfactory pace with their own resources, but which have to correct the persistent trend towards external imbalance so they can convert part of these resources into imports of capital and other goods needed for their economic development. At the other extreme are the countries which are only beginning to develop, and there the top priority is to obtain international finance, most especially for building up their generally weak economic infrastructure and for basically important social investments. The countries which are at an incipient stage of development may possibly not have to contend with an acute persistent imbalance as do the former, since this imbalance is a consequence of development; but it would be advisable to act now to prevent this from occurring in the future by guiding their development, and particularly their industrialization policy, along rational lines, both by import substitution within groupings of countries and by the promotion of exports of manufactures.

In the course of time, the more advanced of the developing countries should be able to provide a market for exports of manufactures from countries which are embarking on the first stages of industrialization by according them preferential treatment.

In all of this there is no master plan, drawn up once and for all, that is equally applicable to all countries. That is why this policy is necessarily a complex one. Furthermore, it must respond and adapt itself continually to endless changes.

New Problems and New Attitudes

Such are the issues for which this Conference must seek international solutions in support of internal endeavour. They are solutions which must be embodied in a new policy, not necessarily in response to new ideas—for the ideas presented here are not fundamentally new—but because they demand new attitudes. Will it be possible to bring about these new attitudes? Will the proposals formulated here be realistic? If realism means proposing what is feasible at a given moment, then perhaps not all that is suggested in these pages is realistic; it might be considered an illusion. But what is realistic today was not always so yesterday, and today's illusion may be tomorrow's realism.

Nothing is more significant in this connexion than the way in which ideas have evolved in the short time that has elapsed since the proposal to hold this Conference was adopted by the United Nations.

Again, reality is made up not just of the tangible facts which we have before us now, but also of the facts still to unfold. Realism is, moreover, the ability to discern what could happen when we do not know how, or do not wish, to take deliberate and timely action to shape the course of events.

The prospects facing the developing countries are grave indeed. Development is turning inwards in the countries that have made more headway in the industrialization process; it is closeting itself more and more in watertight compartments; and the same thing will happen in the others, the less advanced, if they too have to become industrialized within the narrow confines of their national markets. What is more, those countries in general, and the less advanced of them in particular, are not obtaining sufficient financial resources from abroad. These resources are indispensable for breaking that other vicious circle in which incomes are low because investments are inadequate and investments are inadequate because incomes are precarious.

The developing countries must not be forced to cut down the inherently very low consumption of the masses in order to increase capital formation, particularly in view of the impressive magnitude of their aspirations for social betterment. It is no good to preach the need for them to develop by their own efforts and at the same time to limit their possibilities of giving practical expression to that effort in the international field through the expansion of their exports. They must not be forced into a kind of closed development. Hence a broad policy of international co-operation in trade, in financial resources and in the propagation of technology is unavoidable. Without it the economic and social cost of development will be enormous. Closed development leads to compulsion, and usually compulsion involves a political cost fraught with very serious consequences. Realism is also foresight, and an elementary sense of foresight should induce us to read the sign of the times in the developing world.

These pages are therefore an act of faith: an act of faith in the possibility of persuading, of making these ideas sink in where they should sink in, and in the possibility of provoking constructive reactions. The facts are there and cannot be denied. And if the ways of dealing with them proposed here are not acceptable, others will have to be sought which are. For the problem is inescapable. Never before has the world been faced with it in this form and on this scale, nor has it ever had the enormous possibilities that it now has of solving it, or the conviction which is steadily growing—that it is also feasible consciously and deliberately to influence technical and economic forces in the prosecution of grand designs.

4 The Role of the Military

Because of our highly developed tradition of civilian control we in the Western nations tend to regard political activity on the part of the military as undesirable per se. Consequently we have tended to hold this same attitude in judging the situations facing less developed countries and to decry intervention by the military in the affairs of these nations. This is not only ethnocentric but in many cases unrealistic. Even in Latin America, which evokes negative images of political violence and instability, the military can play an important role in the reforms necessitated by the modernization process. In fact, the military may serve as the spearhead of reform. Excellent examples of this role played by the military are offered by the Ayub Khan government in Pakistan and the Gamal Abdel Nasser government in Egypt. In Pakistan the new military government, after banning parties and parliament, systematically restructured Pakistani political institutions from the village level up. In Egypt the military went even further, becoming a revolutionary movement in itself with an ideology and a program for large-scale social transformation. In other instances—in Turkey and Brazil—the military has acted as a temporary caretaker or as the silent backer of a civilian regime.

It is important to emphasize that the military can perform many useful functions in national life other than that of providing national security both without and within. For example, in a new nation where the coefficient of nationalism is low, the army can serve as a nationalizing agent. In others it can provide the chief, if not the only, source of trained administrative and engineering skills. In still others it can offer leadership untainted with charges of corruption, nepotism, and maladministration. But most important, the military can act as a force for political stability and reform in regions where no other sectors of society are able or willing to provide either.

Of course, a central role for the military in the politics of any country should be regarded as only a temporary, transitional state of affairs—a condition that exists to be terminated. Also there is inherent in military intervention the danger of excess. At best, the military is a sharp-edged tool that must be employed carefully, lest it become a permanent fixture on the political scene. In spite of these several caveats it is nevertheless appropriate for us to consider the potentialities of the military in the developmental process. The first selection raises some of the underlying theoretical aspects of this problem. The second and third selections provide illustrations of situations in which the military can make direct practical contributions to the developmental process.

Armies in the Process of Political Modernization

by LUCIAN W. PYE

Only a few years ago it was generally assumed that the future of the newly emergent states would be determined largely by the activities of their Westernized intellectuals, their socialistically inclined bureaucrats, their nationalist ruling parties, and possibly their menacing Communist parties. It occurred to few students of the underdeveloped regions that the military might become the critical group

SOURCE: Reprinted from *The Role of the Military in Underdeveloped Countries*, edited by John J. Johnson, by permission of Princeton University Press. Copyright © 1962, The RAND Corporation. All rights reserved. No part of this book may be reproduced in any form without permission in writing from the publisher.

in shaping the course of nation-building. Now that the military has become the key decision-making element in at least eight of the Afro-Asian countries, we are confronted with the awkward fact that there has been almost no scholarly research on the role of the military in the political development of the new states.

Lack of Knowledge or Doctrine

The trend of recent years toward increased authoritarian rule and army-dominated governments raises questions which seem only to emphasize the limitations of our knowledge. Is it true, as we have always supposed, that any encroachment of the military into civilian rule is a blow to liberal government and civil liberties? Or is it possible that military rule can, in fact, establish the necessary basis for the growth of effective representative institutions? Have events reached such a state in parts of Asia that we should welcome army rule as the least odious of possible developments and probably the only effective counterforce to communism?[1] We seem to be confronted by two conflicting images of the politician in uniform. The first, derived largely from Latin America and the Balkans, is that of administrative incompetence, inaction, and authoritarian, if not reactionary, values. The second and more recent is that of a dynamic and self-sacrificing military leadership committed to progress and the task of modernizing transitional societies that have been subverted by the "corrupt practices" of politicians. How is it possible to tell in any particular case whether army rule will lead to sterile authoritarianism or to vigorous development?

To answer such questions is to explore two relatively unknown and overlapping areas; Western scholarship has been peculiarly inattentive to the sociology of armies, on the one hand, and to the processes of political development and nation-building, on the other. Only in recent years, as Professor William T. R. Fox observed, has the Western scholar's bias against the military been weakened to the point where he is prepared to go beyond the field of civil-

[1] Guy J. Pauker, "Southeas Asia as a Problem Area in the Next Decade," *World Politics,* Vol. XI, No. 3, April 1959, pp. 325–345.

military relations and recognize the entire range of national security problems as a respectable province of scholarship.[2] Given the hesitation with which we have approached the study of the primary functions of armies it is not surprising that so little systematic thought has been given to the political sociology of armies and the roles that military institutions play in facilitating the processes of industrial and political development. It is hardly necessary to document the fact that we have limited knowledge about the nature of political development in transitional societies and the processes that produce the emerging political institutions. Without greater knowledge of these developments we lack perspective for viewing the rise of authoritarian practices and the emergence of military rule in transitional societies.

Our lack of knowledge about such important matters is probably less significant than the fact that we also lack an appropriate doctrine that, in lieu of tested knowledge, might serve to guide our policy. To put the matter bluntly, for all our commitment to democratic values, we do not know what is required for a society to move from a traditional and authoritarian basis to the establishment of democratic institutions and representative institutions.

When this problem has arisen in the past with respect to colonialism, our typical response has been anti-intellectual and anti-rational: colonial powers should relinquish their authority, and then an automatic and spontaneous emergence of democratic practices and institutions could be expected. Unfortunately, with the passing of colonialism we find we have little advice to give to the leaders of the newly emergent countries who are struggling to realize democratic ways. We have no doctrine to offer them, no strategies for action nor criteria of priorities, no sense of appropriate programs nor sets of hypotheses for explaining the paths to representative government. At best we have been able to piece together some concepts and considerations taken from embryonic theories of economic growth and have suggested that they might serve as guiding principles.

[2] Conference on Political Modernization, Social Science Research Council, Committee on Comparative Politics, Dobbs Ferry, June 8–12, 1959.

In contrast to our own bemusement, those interested in establishing other types of social and political systems—and most particularly, of course, the Communists—have a clearer sense of design and of priorities to guide their efforts. More often than not we have found that instead of developmental concepts and strategic plans we can offer only statements about the nature of democratic values and our vision of end-goals of political development. By stressing ends rather than the means we have inadvertently tended to highlight the extent to which the newly emergent states have failed to realize in practice their aspirations. In so doing we have contributed to the growing feeling of insecurity common to most of the leaders of such countries. These are generally men who, despite their bold exteriors, are inwardly plagued with self-doubts and uncertainties about their ability to run a country. Without clear notions as to the stages that must be passed through if their transitional societies are to realize free institutions, these leaders are in danger of thinking that the gap between current performance and democratic ideals means that their peoples are doomed to failure.

Our lack of doctrine for building a tolerably free society is most conspicuous with respect to the proper role of authority in government. How should the machinery of state, usually inherited from an essentially authoritarian colonial regime, be employed to ensure political development? Can these essentially coercive instruments of the state, which in a democratic order are the servants of the popular will, be utilized to guide a tradition-bound people to democratic values and habits of thought? Or is the result of any such efforts, no matter how well intended, likely to be a drift toward what is essentially an authoritarian order decorated with democratic trimmings? It would seem that these questions might serve as an appropriate beginning for a search for both a doctrine of political tutelage and a better understanding of the role of the military in the process of political modernization.

An underlying assumption behind much of Western political thought is that political institutions are above all else the products of the dynamic forces peculiar to a particular society and thus reflect the distinctive values and the styles of action common to that society. It is acknowledged, of course, that once institutions are established they tend to become dynamic and hence influence the values and the expectations of the population. There is thus an assumption of a circularity of relationships or a state of equilibrium. The fundamental view, however, is still that the dynamics of the system lie within the society as a whole and that it is the institutions which must be responsive. Governmental institutions can display initiative, but fundamental change originates within the society.

When we turn to the newly emergent countries this model no longer seems appropriate. For in these societies the historical pattern has been the introduction of institutions from outside, with a minimum concession to the values and behavior of the people. These fundamentally authoritative structures have thus tended to be shaped according to foreign standards. Rather than responding to indigenous values they have often proved to be the dominant factor in stimulating further changes throughout the society.

These considerations suggest that it might be useful to organize our analysis of the political role of the army, first, with respect to the political implications of the army as a modern institution that has been somewhat artificially introduced into disorganized transitional societies; and second, with respect to the role that such an army can play in shaping attitudes toward modernity in other spheres of society. By such an approach we may hope to locate some of the critical factors for explaining why it is that the military has been a vigorous champion of progress and development in some countries and a retarding influence in others. We may also hope to gain a basis for judging the probable effectiveness of armies in promoting national development and eventually democratic practices.

The Army as a Modern Organization

In large measure the story of the underdeveloped countries is one of countless efforts to create organizations by which resources can be effectively mobilized for achieving new objectives. This is the problem of establishing organizations that, as rationalized structures, are capable of relating means to ends. The history of much of the Western impact on traditional societies fits comfortably within this theme, for the businessman, planter, and miner, the colonial administrator, the missionary, and the educator each in his own way strives to fit modern organizations into tradition-bound societies. Similarly, the story of the nationalists and of the other Westernized leaders can be treated on essentially identical terms, for they too try to change the habits of their people by creating modern organizations.

Needless to say, there are not many bright spots in this history, and it is open to question as to who has been the more tragically heroic or comically futile: the Westerners struggling to establish their organizations in traditional societies, or the nationalist politician and the indigenous administrator endeavoring to create a semblance of order out of chaos. On balance, the attempts to establish military organizations seem to have been noticeably the most successful.

It would be wrong to underestimate the patient care that has gone into developing and training colonial armies, and in the newly independent countries the military have been treated relatively generously in the allocation of scarce resources. But in comparison to the efforts that have been expended in developing, say, civil administration and political parties, it still seems that modern armies are somewhat easier to create in transitional societies than are most other forms of modern social structures. The significant fact for our consideration is that the armies created by colonial administration and by the newly emergent countries have been consistently among the most modernized institutions in their societies. Viewed historically, some of these armies have been distinguished: the Indian Army, the Malay Regiments, the Philippine Scouts, the Arab Legion, the Gurkha Regiments, and the King's Own African Rifles, to mention only the more celebrated ones.

It would take us too far afield to explore the relative advantages military leaders have in seeking to establish armies in transitional societies. We need only note that there is a paradoxical relationship between ritualized and rationalized modes of behavior that may account for the ease with which people still close to a traditional order adapt themselves to military life. Viewed from one perspective, a military establishment comes as close as any human organization can to the ideal type for an industrialized and secularized enterprise. Yet from another point of view, the great stress placed on professionalism and the extremely explicit standards for individual behavior make the military appear to be a more sacred than secular institution. If discipline is needed to minimize random and unpredictable behavior, it is also consonant with all the demands that custom and ritual make in the most tradition-bound organization.

For these reasons, and for others related to the hierarchic nature of the organization, the division between traditional and rationally oriented behavior is not very great within armies.[3] Indeed, in any army there is always a struggle going on between tradition and reason. Historically, during periods of little change in the state of military technology the tendency has been for the nonrational characteristics to become dominant.[4] Given this inherent conflict in any military organization the question arises as to why the forces of custom and ritual do not readily dominate the armies of the newly emergent countries, and so cause them to oppose the forces of change. In societies where traditional habits of mind are still strong one might expect the military to be strongly conservative. Such was largely the case in the West during the preindustrial period. By contrast, in most of the newly emergent countries armies have tended to emphasize a rational outlook and to champion responsible change and national development.

This state of affairs is largely explained by the extent to which the armies in these countries have been influenced by contemporary Western military technology. In particular, nearly all of the new

[3] It is significant that the most common weaknesses of civil bureaucracies in the new countries—like exaggerating the importance of procedure to the point of ritualizing the routine, and the lack of initiative and of a pragmatic and experimental outlook—are not as serious drawbacks to smooth functioning of military establishment. On the contrary, the very qualities that have hobbled civil administration in these countries have given strength and rigidity to their military establishments.

[4] The classic discussion of the spirit of militarism as contrasted with the rational military mind is Alfred Vagts, *A History of Militarism: Romance and Realities of a Profession*, New York, 1937.

countries have taken the World War II type of army as their model.[5] In so doing they have undertaken to create a form of organization that is typical of and peculiar to the most highly industrialized civilization yet known. Indeed, modern armies are essentially industrial-type entities. Thus the armies of the new countries are instinct with the spirit of rapid technological development.

The fact that these new armies in preindustrial societies are modeled after industrial-based organizations has many implications for their political roles. One of their characteristics is particularly significant: the specialization that modern armies demand in skills and functions is only distantly related to the command of violence. There has generally been a tremendous increase in the number of officers assigned to staff functions as contrasted with line commands. As the armies have striven to approximate their ideal models they have had to establish all manner of specialized organizations and departments that require skills that are either in short supply or nonexistent in their societies. The Burmese Army, for example, in addition to its engineer and signal corps has special sections on chemical warfare, psychological warfare, and even a historical and archaeological section. All the new armies have attempted to introduce specialized training schools and advanced techniques of personnel management and procurement. Consequently, numbers of the more intelligent and ambitious officers have had to be trained in industrial skills more advanced than those common to the civilian economy.

The high proportion of officers assigned to staff functions means that large numbers of officers are forced to look outside their society for their models. The fact that army leaders, particularly the younger and more ambitious, generally come from those trained in staff positions means that they are extremely sensitive to the needs of modernization and technological advancement. This kind of sensi-

[5] World War II was in itself a decisive event in the birth of many of these countries and, of course, the availability of large quantities of surplus equipment and arms made it realistic to aspire to a modernized army. American military aid has contributed to making the military the most modernized element in not only recipient countries, but also in neighboring countries which have felt the need to keep up with technological advances.

tivity bears little relationship to the command of physical violence and tests of human endurance—in short, to the martial spirit as we customarily think of it. In consequence the officers often find that they are spiritually in tune with the intellectuals, students, and those other elements in society most anxious to become a part of the modern world. They may have little in common with the vast majority of the men they must command. In this respect the gap between the officer class and the troops, once largely a matter of social and economic class (as it still is to some degree), has now been widened by differences in the degree of acculturation to modern life.

It should be noted that these revolutionary changes in military life have significantly influenced the status of the military profession in different societies and hence have had an interesting effect on relative national power. Cultures that looked down on the military at an earlier stage of technology now accord high prestige to the same profession as it has raised its technology. For example, when armies depended entirely on human energy and animal power the Chinese placed the soldier near the bottom of the social hierarchy; with present levels of advanced military technology the soldier is now near the top of the social scale in both Communist and non-Communist China. The change has been more in the nature of the military profession than in basic Chinese cultural values. Conversely, peoples once considered "martial" may now show little interest in, or aptitude for, the new kind of soldiering.

Above all else, however, the revolution in military technology has caused the army leaders of the newly emergent countries to be extremely sensitive to the extent to which their countries are economically and technologically underdeveloped. Called upon to perform roles basic to advanced societies, the more politically conscious officers can hardly avoid being aware of the need for substantial changes in their own societies.

It might seem that those occupying positions in other modern-type organizations in underdeveloped societies would also feel much the same need for change. To whatever extent this may be so, three distinctive features of armies seem to make them somewhat more dynamic in demanding changes.

93

First of all, armies by nature are rival institutions in the sense that their ultimate function is the test of one against the other. All other organizations operate within the context of their own society; although their initial inspiration may have come from abroad, their primary focus is on internal developments. The civil bureaucracy, for example, can, and indeed has to, deal with its domestic problems with little regard for what other bureaucracies in other countries are doing. The soldier, however, is constantly called upon to look abroad and to compare his organization with foreign ones. He thus has a greater awareness of international standards and a greater sensitivity to weaknesses in his own society.

Second, armies for all their concern with rationality and becoming highly efficient machines are relatively immune to pragmatic tests of efficiency on a day-to-day basis. Armies are created for future contingencies, and in many underdeveloped countries these contingencies have never had to be faced. Even in countries such as Burma and Indonesia, where the army is forced to deal with internal security problems, the effects have been mainly to increase the resources available for building up the army according to the ideal model, with remarkably few concessions being made to practical needs. Other modernized organizations in underdeveloped societies have to cope with more immediate and day-to-day problems; hence they must constantly adjust themselves to local conditions. They cannot adhere as rigidly as armies can to their Western prototypes. Just as Western armies have often existed in a dream world of planning for types of wars that never occur, so armies of underdeveloped countries can devote themselves to becoming modernized and more "efficient" with little regard to immediate reality. Members of other modern-type organizations may desire to see social change in their society, but they are likely to be more conscious of the need to accommodate their ambitions to existing conditions.

Finally, armies always stand at some distance from their civilian societies and are even expected to have ways of their own, including attitudes and judgments, that are remote if not completely apart from those of civilian life. Thus again armies of the newly emergent countries can feel somewhat divorced from the realities of a transitional society and focus more on the standards common to the more industrialized world. In consequence they are often unaware of the difficulties inherent in modernizing other segments of their society. Within their tradition all problems can be overcome if the right orders are given.

Armies as Modernizing Agents

So much for the army as one of the more modernized of the authoritative agencies of government in transitional societies. When we consider it as a modernizing force for the whole of society, we move into a less clearly defined area where the number of relevant considerations becomes much greater and where we are likely to find greater differences from country to country. Indeed, we shall be able to deal only generally with the social and political aspects of military service and some of the more indirect influences of armies on civilian attitudes.

In all societies it is recognized that armies must make those who enter them into the image of the good soldier. The underdeveloped society adds a new dimension: the good soldier is also to some degree a modernized man. Thus it is that the armies in the newly emergent countries come to play key roles in the process by which traditional ways give way to more Westernized ideas and practices. The very fact that the recruit must break his ties and associations with civilian life and adjust to the more impersonal world of the army tends to emphasize the fundamental nature of this process, which involves the movement out of the particularistic relationships of traditional life and into the more impersonal and universalistic relationships of an industrialized society.

Army training is thus consistent with the direction taken by the basic process of acculturation in traditional societies. Within the army, however, the rate of acculturation is greatly accelerated. This fact contributes to the tendency of army officers to underestimate the difficulties of changing the civilian society.

Probably the most significant feature of the acculturation process as it takes place under the auspices of the army is that it provides a relatively high degree of psychological security. The experience of breaking from the known and relatively sheltered world of tradition and moving into the more unknown modern world is generally an extremely traumatic one. In contrast to the villager who is caught up in the process of being urbanized, the young army recruit from the village has the more sheltered, the more gradual introduction into the modern world. It is hardly necessary to point out the disturbing fact that the urbanization process as it has taken place in most Asian, African, and Latin-American societies has generally tended to produce a highly restless, insecure population. Those who have been forced off the land or attracted to the cities often find themselves in a psychologically threatening situation. These are the people who tend to turn to extremist politics and to look for some form of social and personal security in political movements that demand their total commitment. In contrast, those who are exposed to a more technologically advanced way of life in the army find that they must make major adjustments, but that these adjustments are all treated explicitly and openly. In the army one can see what is likely to happen in terms of one's training and one's future. This is not the case in the city.

It should also be noted that the acculturative process in the army often tends to be more thorough and of a broader scope than the urbanization process. In all the main Asian cities there are those who still follow many of the habits and practices of the village. They may live still within the orbit of their family and have only limited outside associations and contacts. These people have made some adjustment to the modern world, but they are likely to be faced with even more in the future, and thus they remain potential sources of political tension.

It should also be noted that the acculturative process in the army tends to be focused on acquiring technical skills that are of particular value for economic development. Just as the army represents an industrialized organization, so must those who have been trained within it learn skills and habits of mind which would be of value in other industrial organizations. In the West, armies have played a very important role in providing technical training and even direct services in the process of industrial development. The German Army trained large numbers of non-commissioned officers who performed important functions as foremen in the German steel mills and in other industries. In the United States the Corps of Engineers, of course, played a central role in the whole development of the West; and, after the Civil War, army veterans provided considerable amounts of the skill and knowledge which, when combined with the influx of immigrants, provided a basis for much of our industrial development. In Latin America the Brazilian Army has played an important part in opening the interior, in promoting the natural sciences, and in protecting the Indian population. In Asia, too, we can see much the same story being enacted now. Before the war the compulsory training in the Japanese Army provided the whole society with increasing reservoirs of manpower which contributed directly to the development of an industrial society. Army veterans in India have played an important role not only in lower-level industrial jobs, but also in managerial positions. In Malaya and the Philippines the army has been the main instrument for training people in operating and maintaining motor vehicles and other forms of machinery.

Politically the most significant feature of the process of acculturation within the army is that it usually provides some form of training in citizenship. Recruits with traditional backgrounds must learn about a new world in which they are identified with a larger political self. They learn that they stand in some definite relationship to a national community. In this sense the army experience tends to be a politicizing experience. Even if recruits are not given explicit training in political matters, they are likely to learn that events in their society are determined by human decisions and not just by chance and fate. Within the army the peasant may come to realize that much in life can be changed and that commands and wishes have consequences. Thus even aside from any formal training in patriotism the recruit is likely to achieve some awareness of the political dimensions of his society. It is therefore not surprising that in many of the newly emergent countries veterans have had appreciable political influence even after only limited military experience.

97

Armies in the newly emergent countries can thus provide a sense of citizenship and an appreciation of political action. In some cases this can lead to a more responsible nationalism. Indeed, the recruit may be impressed with the fact that he must make sacrifices to achieve the goals of nationalism and that the process of nation-building involves more than just the shouting of slogans. At the same time there is always the potential danger that the armies will become the center of hypernationalistic movements, as in the case of prewar Japan.

Because the army represents one of the most effective channels for upward social mobility, military-inspired nationalism often encompasses a host of personalized emotions and sentiments about civilian society. Invariably the men, and sometimes even the officers, come from extremely humble circumstances, and it is only within the army that they are first introduced to the possibility of systematically advancing themselves. In transitional societies, where people's station in life is still largely determined by birth and by chance opportunities, powerful reactions usually follow from placing people in a position where they can recognize a definite and predictable relationship between effort and reward. The practice of giving advancement on merit can encourage people, first, to see the army as a just organization deserving of their loyalties, and then possibly, to demand that the same form of justice reign throughout their society.

Those who do move up to positions of greater respect and power through the army may often carry with them hostilities toward those with greater advantages and authority in civilian society. The tendency of the military to question whether the civilian elite achieved their station by merit adds another conflict to civil-military relations in most underdeveloped countries. More often than not the military show these feelings by seeking to make national loyalty and personal sacrifice the crucial test of national leadership.

The relationship between armies and civilian leaders varies, of course, according to the circumstances of historic development. For this reason a large part of this volume is devoted to case studies. Broadly speaking, however, it is helpful to distinguish three different general categories of such relationships.

There are first those patterns of development in which the military stand out because in a disrupted society they represent the only effectively organized element capable of competing for political power and formulating public policy. This situation is most likely to exist when the traditional political order, but not necessarily the traditional social order, has been violently disrupted and it becomes necessary to set up representative institutions before any of the other modern-type political organizations have been firmly established. The outstanding example of this pattern of development is modern China from the fall of the Manchu dynasty in 1911 to the victory of the Communists. Indeed, it is possible to think of this period as one dominated by a constant struggle to escape from the grim circumstances that obtained when only military organizations survived the fall of the traditional systems. Hence the military became the only effective political entity. Thereafter nothing could be done without them, and yet the military could do little without effective civilian institutions. Comparable situations seem to exist at present in some Middle Eastern countries where Western influence brought a commitment to republican institutions but left the army as the only effective modern political structure in the entire society.

A second category includes those countries where the military, while formally espousing the development of democracy, actually monopolizes the political arena and forces any emerging civilian elite to concentrate on economic and social activities. In many ways this arrangement is reminiscent of the Belgian variety of colonialism. At present, the most outstanding example of this form of rule is Thailand.

A third major category, which is probably the largest, consists of those countries in which the organization and structures essential to democratic government exist but have not been able to function effectively. The process of modernization has been retarded to such a point that the army, as the most modernized organization in the society, has assumed an administrative role and taken over control. In these cases there is a sense of failure in the country, and the military are viewed as possible saviors.

Before turning to our case studies, it is appropriate to note briefly some of the broader implications of the role of the armies in transitional countries—particularly in terms of international stability. The ways in which new societies are being created will have profound significance for the entire world. At the same time it is unrealistic to conclude that the army's role in the new countries is determined only by domestic developments. The nature of the contemporary international order and the focus of Western policies have had a profound influence on military institutions throughout the underdeveloped areas.

There has been a tendency in some quarters to regard the trend toward military rule as favorable to American policy interests. In particular, army rule has been welcomed as promising greater political stability and firmer policies against communism. Unfortunately, in the past we have generally been poor judges of leadership in the new countries. In fact, we have been so anxious to wish the new countries well that we have not been very realistic in appraising their national leadership. We have often placed faith in, and indeed lionized, men who are mediocre by any standard of measurement. The fault is more serious than just a misplaced sense of charitableness, for by refusing to employ realistic standards of judgment we encourage the lack of realism and even quackery in the political life of many of these countries.

In seeking a realistic estimate of the potential role of the military in the political development of particular countries it is also necessary to avoid being excessively influenced by ideological considerations which may be relevant only in advanced societies. We have in mind, in particular, the Western stereotype of the military as a foe of liberal values. This bias, for example, tends at present to take the form of seeing "military aid" as a threat to economic and political development and of assuming that only "economic aid" can make a positive contribution to such form of development. In some cases military aid has in fact made substantial contributions to road building, health facilities, communications networks and the like, all of which have directly facilitated economic growth. In other cases it has been equally clear that our military aid has seriously retarded economic development by diverting an excessive amount of the nation's energies into unproductive channels. The point is only that in our thinking about the newly emergent countries we must avoid stereotypes and expect many paradoxes.

If we are able to do so, we will be less surprised to note, for example, that it has been through the military that we have best been able to establish effective relations with the most strongly neutralist nations in Southeast Asia. With both Burma and Indonesia we have had considerable difficulties in almost every dimension of our relationships. Recently, however, it has appeared that we have been able to develop more genuine and straightforward relations with their military than with any other political element. Out of these relations have come further possibilities for cooperation. Thus, rather ironically, after the Burmese terminated our program of economic assistance to them, it was possible to reestablish such assistance only by first providing them with military aid. In this way confidence was reestablished and the stage set for their reacceptance of economic aid.

This particular example may, in fact, point up a most important consideration about armies in the new countries. For the various reasons which we have mentioned the army is often the most modernized public organization in an underdeveloped country, and as a consequence its leaders often feel more self-confident and are more able to deal frankly and cordially with representatives of industrialized countries. Military leaders are often far less suspicious of the West than civilian leaders because they themselves are more emotionally secure. This sense of security makes it possible for army leaders to look more realistically at their countries. All of these considerations make it easier for the military leaders to accept the fact that their countries are weak and the West is strong without becoming emotionally disturbed or hostile toward the West. Since these leaders seem to have less need to avoid realities, they are in fact easier people with whom to deal and to carry on straightforward relations.

It is important, however, to note from the example that it is possible, and indeed it is essential, to expand a narrow relationship with the military into a much broader one. Military aid has had to become economic aid. Satisfactory relations with the military can become a dead end, just as military rule itself can become sterile if it does not lead to an interest in total national development.

This is only to say that while it may be possible to find in the armies of underdeveloped countries an element of stability, we should not confuse this with political stability for the entire society. The military may provide an opportunity and a basis for cooperation, but the objective must remain the development of stable representative institutions and practices. In planning for this objective it is essential to conceive of it as involving far more than just the efficient administration of public policies. It is necessary to keep in mind that in the past the West has come to these societies largely in the guise of administrators. This was the nature of colonialism, and we have tended to step into this role with our emphasis upon economic aid. In cooperating with the military we again are essentially strengthening this role of the administrator. In most underdeveloped countries there is at present a genuine need to improve the standards of public administration. In fact, unless such improvements take place they will be able to realize few of their national goals. However, there is a deeper problem, and this is the problem of developing effective relations between the administrators and the politicians. The disturbing fact is that we can with relative ease help people perform administrative roles, but we have not been particularly successful in devising ways of training people to the role of the democratic politician. In many respects this difficulty is the heart of the problem in our relations with the new countries.

This leads us to the conclusion that the military in the underdeveloped countries can make a major contribution to strengthening essentially administrative functions. If the new countries are to become modern nation-states they will have to have a class of competent administrators. They will also have to have responsible and skilled politicians. In cooperating with the military in these countries we should therefore recognize that they can contribute to only a limited part of national development. In particular, in assisting them to raise standards in the realm of public administration, we should also make certain that our assistance does not lead to a stifling of an even more basic aspect of political development: the growth of responsible and representative politicians.

Military Civic Action

edited by RICHARD M. LEIGHTON
and RALPH SANDERS

"The new generation of military leaders has shown an increasing awareness that armies can not only defend their countries—they can help to build them." Thus did President Kennedy, in an address to the Diplomatic Corps of the Latin American countries in March 1961, express the role which military forces can play in a program now widely known as civic action.

This definition of civic action is: "The use of preponderantly indigenous military forces on projects useful to the local population at all levels in such fields as education, training, public works, agriculture, transportation, communications, health, sanitation and others contributing to economic and social development, which would also serve to improve the standing of the military forces with the population. (U.S. Forces may at times advise or engage in military civic actions in overseas areas)."

Because of the very nature of military civic action, most activities associated with this work take place within the boundaries of emerging and developing nations far from the U.S. shores. Consequently, few U.S. citizens have the opportunity to observe these activities in operation or evaluate their results. The Services and agencies working in military civic action have found it necessary to tailor their activities and programs to the economic, political and sociological structure of each country involved and to the aims and interest of the United States in each area. We are trying to use the best methods—the best ideas—the best programs in each situation. But we are constantly in search of fresh ideas—new approaches and

SOURCE: *New Dimensions in the Cold War,* edited by Richard M. Leighton and Ralph Sanders (Washington, D.C.: Industrial College of the Armed Forces, 1963). The selection reprinted here is Chapter 11, which was prepared by the Civil Affairs Directorate, Deputy Chief of Staff for Military Operations, Department of the Army.

program refinement, particularly when dealing with the problem of establishing a cooperative, reciprocal attitude between a country's military and civilian elements.

Background

In the restive two-thirds of the world, which we call underdeveloped, insurgency is a present incipient problem because of social inequities, political instability and Communist subversion. There is a desire on the part of the people of these countries for a better way of life. This is the battleground of the cold war. We must recognize that in any battle for control of an area the people must be considered and the side that wins support of the people will win the battle. Dr. Franklin Lindsay, writing on unconventional warfare in the *Foreign Affairs* Quarterly for January 1962, has very aptly stated the principle by saying, "Just as control of the air has become a prerequisite for successful frontal warfare, so control of the population is a prerequisite for successful unconventional warfare." Military civic action is one of the valuable ways of gaining that necessary control.

The military civic action program is based on the premise that the capabilities of military forces can be used to make a significant contribution to economic and social development in the less developed countries and in so doing gain better support of the people for the military and the government it represents. This concept is based on legislation which was placed in the basic act of the U.S. Congress on economic and military assistance in 1959. This was carried over and included in the new Act for International Development of 1961, which is the current legislation for administration of the economic and military assistance program. Sec. 505b of this act provides:

To the extent feasible . . . the use of military forces in less developed, friendly countries in the construction of public works, and other activities helpful to economic development shall be encouraged.

An overall policy pronouncement made at the executive level of the Government indicated that we may not be doing enough in this field and defined three types of situations where military civic action would be useful.

a. In countries fighting active campaigns against internal subversion, military civic action is an indispensable means of strengthening the economic base and establishing a link between armed forces and the populace.

b. In countries threatened by external aggression, forces should participate in civic action projects which do not materially impair performance of the primary military mission.

c. In countries where subversion or attack is less imminent, selected indigenous military forces can contribute substantively to economic and social development, and such a contribution can be a major function of these forces.

Military civic action should be looked upon as both a preventive or countering measure to help prevent deterioration in a country, and also as a technique of guerrilla and counterguerrilla warfare. Guerrilla warfare can never be effective unless it is supported, or at least passively accepted, by the people of the area. To fight subversion and insurgency, the forces of a nation must win the people to their side. The forces must recognize that the manner in which they behave toward the people greatly influences the course of events. Civic action, however, must be looked upon not as a substitute for military power, but rather as one element of it—a weapon for combat-capable forces. It is an effective device which such forces, along with other governmental agencies, can use as their contribution to the development and well-being of the people and their areas. Civic action can range anywhere from basic military courtesy and discipline up through formal unit projects.

On 9 October 1962, Secretary of State Rusk at the dedication of facilities for use by the Inter-American Defense College, placed emphasis on the present military civic action program with the following statement:

> I need not emphasize the very substantial political advantages to be realized by a wholehearted expansion in the military civic action program. I would suggest that the full range of activities possible under joint civic action programs be made a main field of study by the Inter-American Defense College.
>
> The ultimate solution to the problems that face us today will be the achievement of political, economic, and social stability under democratic

institutions. All elements of society have a role in this solution, the military forces most importantly so. It is toward this end that we all must work.

It is the indigenous forces of a country we need to reach to encourage them to use their capabilities on those programs which will have the greatest impact on the people. Therefore, we must put the burden for accomplishment of this objective on the U.S. Country Team in each country, which consists of the Ambassador, the Chief of the U.S. Military Mission or Military Group, and, among others, representatives of the Agency for International Development and United States Information Service. The Ambassador, as head of the team must furnish the necessary drive and guidance and direction for all of the elements of his team. In the development of the program and its funding, the two most important elements of the team are the Agency for International Development and the Military Assistance Advisory Group or Military Mission people. The Agency for International Development in each country is the Ambassador's chief agency for the economic assistance given the country. Therefore, the military civic action program must complement and not compete with that program. Civilian agencies, however, have certain limitations in coping with remote areas and insurgency situations, while military forces have corresponding advantages.

One advantage of military agencies is their ability to send highly qualified specialists to areas for which it would be extremely difficult to recruit qualified civilians. Further, these military specialists are available in nearly every field of activity. Some examples of specialist talents in the Army are found in the fields of health, education, public works, agronomy, transportation, safety, construction, and administration.

There are several fields of activity where the military can make a significant civic action contribution. Five of these are basic: (a) sanitation and public health, (b) communications, (c) engineering, (d) resettlement, and (e) education.

The entire field of sanitation, public health, and basic medical assistance is one where needs are great and where the military can give assistance.

There is a serious lack of means of communication in most areas and the military has an extensive capability to assist in overcoming this shortage.

One of the greatest shortages is in the area of engineering skills. Assistance can be given in building simple roads, bridges, water systems, civic buildings, and many other needed facilities.

Resettlement is essential in opening new areas in many countries.

Improvement of the educational level of a population is basic to the achievement of sociological, economic, and possibly political improvement.

In the military, our representative on the country team is the Chief, Military Assistance Advisory Group, or Chief, Military Mission, who administers the military assistance program for the Ambassador. Our objective has been to give the Military Assistance Advisory Group or Mission all possible help in encouraging and developing the military civic action program. There are two primary ways we do this—by providing on the Military Assistance Advisory Group staff, permanently assigned personnel with the technical skills required to assist in planning and implementing a civic action program; and by organizing and sending to the Military Assistance Advisory Group specialist teams qualified to plan and put into effect a military civic action program. These civic action mobile training teams are sent on a temporary duty basis at the request of the country team and the concurrence of the country concerned. The mission of these military civic action teams is:

a. Orientation of the Military Assistance Advisory Group or Mission staffs and other members of the country team, as appropriate, on the civic action concept and the role of the Military Assistance Advisory Groups in the program.

b. Survey of the country for needs which can be met through civic action programs.

c. Development of a civic action program for the specific country.

d. When requested by the Military Assistance Advisory Group/ Mission Chief, provide training and guidance for local forces and provide specific technical assistance on projects.

Another technique used to encourage use of military forces on nation building projects is through our school system. Allied officers attend our technical service schools where they become proficient in skills useful in military civic action. They attend the Civil Affairs School and the Special Forces School where the techniques of civic action are taught. In the near future, we plan to have a two-month course on military civic action to be given at the U.S. Army Civil Affairs School which will include U.S. officer as well as Allied officer students. The scope of this course will take in everything from country team organization to the best methods of providing water to a remote village.

We are sometimes faced with a country condition wherein the military have little if any technical capability. To some extent, for example, we found this to be true in Laos. The technique here is to have the indigenous military command form military civic action teams, and using U.S. assets, give them basic skill training in such things as sanitation, administration, and public works. These teams are then sent to a village or rural area to train, guide, and assist as needed. A subsidiary type of program is the literacy and vocational training given to military personnel to give them a skill useful to themselves and the community to which they return upon leaving military service.

There are, of course, many limitations to military civic action programs which must be recognized and considered. One of these is the capabilities of military forces. In many of the underdeveloped areas their capabilities are so low, a basic training program is the first requirement; in others there is an amazing amount of skill to be found, and in all cases there is usually organization and discipline which are necessary to getting a job done. To mention other limitations—most underdeveloped countries have little if any funds to devote to the program; there is always the question of how much the civic action program should be permitted to interfere with the primary military mission and with training for that mission; lastly, it is not always easy to find U.S. military personnel with the necessary area and language knowledge, coupled with technical knowledge needed to give supervision, instruction and guidance.

The relationship in the military civic action program of the military, economic, political, public information, and other fields at the country team level has been previously indicated. This same relationship is essential at the Washington level in the planning and policy formation. In the development of a military civic action program for a specific country, the State Department gives the guidance on the U.S. objectives for that country and determines the political effect of military civic action; the Agency for International Development produces a coordinated economic development program which must be followed in each country with many ramifications such as use of local currency, effect on the employment situation, etc., all of which must be considered when promoting military civic action; the U.S. Information Agency must consider the effect of a military civic action program in its plan for promoting the free world's interest in each country, for informing the people what the military is doing for them; and the military agencies must consider the effect of military civic action on the type and number of forces required for a country, and whether such a program will contribute to the military objective for the country. For the military, the required coordination in programming and funding is accomplished by the Office of the Assistant Secretary of Defense for International Security Affairs.

Prior to sending a military civic action mobile training team to a country, the team is brought into Washington for briefings and consultation with the concerned governmental agencies. The team thus gains an understanding of the related role of these agencies and the policy objectives of each.

It is only during the past few months that a military civic action funding policy has been agreed upon by Department of State, the Agency for International Development, and the Department of Defense. We now have a coordinated program for providing funds through the Military Assistance Program and the Agency for International Development for approved military civic action projects. In the spring of 1960, when the Department of the Army began a concentrated program of encouraging the Military Assistance Advisory Groups and Missions to promote the military civic action program, it was necessary to caution them that the program must be a very low, or no cost, program to the U.S., and also that the projects should be those which could be funded by the country itself. Despite many important projects, it soon became evident that, in some countries, there were absolutely no country funds available for the military civic action projects. It was also evident that even a small amount of U.S. funds to provide such things as handtools and medical supplies would make a great impact upon the country's economy.

With the intensified interest in military civic action resulting from the National Security Council pronouncements, the Departments of Defense and State, and the Agency for International Development developed the present funding formula and transmitted it to the field in a joint State-Defense-Agency for International Development message. This funding formula provides the following:

The Military Assistance Program is now authorized to program and fund for equipment and its maintenance which is used by military and paramilitary units for civic action and for any training connected therewith. The Agency for International Development, on the other hand, is authorized to fund material costs, such as lumber, cement, steel, and other construction items. With this policy, some fiscal year 1962 funds were put into military civic action projects, and for the first time military civic action funds are being programmed for fiscal year 1963.

The military civic action programming, funding, and the assistance being given the country are a coordinated team effort. It is determined at the country level which portion of the funds for a project should come from the Agency for International Development, and which from the Military Assistance Program; who will furnish required technical guidance; whether a civic action mobile training team is required, and in general what method of operation will best accomplish the objectives sought.

In discussing coordination at the Washington and field levels, it may be well to mention a few words on relationships with the Peace Corps. It is obvious that the objectives of the two programs—helping people at the grass roots level—are parallel. We must be very careful, however, not to confuse the military effort with the

Peace Corps effort, or in any way give a military tinge to the Peace Corps. At the Washington level, coordination is maintained with the Peace Corps Headquarters, and at present, there is much useful exchange of information on the two training programs. We must be very careful not to consider the military program as the "military peace corps," which some journalists have done.

We must certainly recognize that the concept of military civic action is not new. In many developing countries, commendable programs have been and are being executed in agriculture, road, bridge, and other building activities, sanitation, resettlement, and other constructive channels. In Korea, the Armed Forces Assistance to Korea program has helped rehabilitate communities. In the Philippines and Burma, the military was one of the principal tools on which the government depended for the establishment of law and order, civic leadership, local improvements and development of virgin areas by settlement.

The program employed by the Philippines to defeat the Huks during the years 1950–53 provides a dramatic success story of a free nation's effort to defeat a Communist-inspired and supported subversive enemy within the country. The key features of President Ramon Magsaysay's campaign were: (a) development of harmonious military-civil relations, (b) military civic action, particularly village level economic development and social improvement, and (c) improved organization and training for combat.

The Armed Forces Assistance to Korea program in Korea has proved to be a highly successful venture combining the efforts of the people and the U.S. Forces. Our forces have given advice and assistance in community development and improvement. Schools, churches, hospitals, irrigation systems, bridges, and roads have been typical projects included in the Armed Forces Assistance to Korea program. Such practical and outgoing concern for Korean welfare has immeasurably improved military-civil relations in Korea, and has won the sincere friendship of the population for our Armed Forces. The Korean forces are now effectively using this same program.

We can safely say now that there are very few underdeveloped, or for that matter, developed countries, where our U.S. Country Team has not heard of the military civic action program and many have taken steps to determine where it can and should fit into their overall program.

Current Status

Turning now to the current Department of the Army military civic action program, during fiscal year 1962, fourteen countries were given U.S. assistance with their programs—nine South and Central American countries and Iran, Jordan, Burma, and the Republics of Vietnam and Korea. Military Assistance Program funding for military civic action in fiscal year 1962 amounted to approximately fourteen million dollars with roughly three million dollars of Agency for International Development funds expended on military civic action type programs.

We have sent civic action mobile training teams to Guatemala, Laos, El Salvador, Iran, Ecuador, the Republics of Korea and Vietnam, Burma, Indonesia, Thailand and Colombia, and have given staff assistance in a number of others. In all, there are at least 28 countries now in various stages of developing or operating a military civic action program where the Country Team has given guidance and assistance.

In the fall of 1961, a trip was made by a Department of the Army team to Ecuador, Guatemala, and Colombia to observe and evaluate the military civic action programs in these countries. This team found the following to be true:

a. In all three countries there is enthusiastic support for the program by the country teams, the officials of the national governments, the military services, and the civilian population.

b. It was apparent in all countries that military civic action has been wholeheartedly adopted as a country team program. Members of the embassy staffs felt that military civic action had welded the country teams together more than any previous U.S. program. This sense of cooperation which pervaded the U.S. country teams seems to extend to the ministries of the local governments. The troop level military-civilian cooperation is an unexpected but sizable dividend of the program.

c. The relationship between the military and the people had improved as a result of military civic action.

d. Military civic action has had no adverse effects on military training and efficiency. The demands of the program are balanced against troop operational and training requirements.

e. In general, it appears that the troops are enjoying their participation in the military civic action program. In many cases, this participation has resulted in giving them a technical capability which they had previously not acquired. For example, they are being trained as bulldozer operators, as assistant surveyors, as bricklayers, and so forth.

The program in Ecuador is presently an active one and is a fine example of how a military civic action program is initiated and carried out.

The Ecuador story properly begins on the 5th of August, 1961, when the American Embassy in Quito informed the Department of State that the Minister of National Defense of Ecuador desired that a civic action mobile training team be sent to Ecuador as soon as possible.

Based on the detailed requirements developed by the Chief of Mission in Ecuador in coordination with the other members of the country team, and submitted through the Unified Commander, the Department of the Army selected the requested military civic action mobile training team. At the conclusion of a period of indoctrination, the team, consisting of a team chief and civil affairs officer, a medical officer, a psychological operations officer, a signal officer and an engineer officer, departed the United States, arriving in Ecuador on 21 January 1962.

Upon arrival in the area of operations, the team immediately undertook a detailed on-the-ground survey to determine the projects which were most needed and which the Ecuadorian military forces could undertake. The team worked closely with representatives and agencies of the country team, their Ecuadorian civilian and military counterparts, and such agencies as the Pan American Health Organization, the Inter-American Cooperative Public Health Service and the Andean Mission.

With the completion of the survey, the team proceeded to draw up a program of action to suit the requirements of the area and the military capabilities. Details of the program were worked up in close coordination with the Agency for International Development and the Ecuadorian military and civilian representatives. Every effort was made to select projects which would have widespread support, and in which local resources and capabilities could be utilized to the maximum degree.

The final program developed contained projects with a cost of about $1.5 million to the United States. It is now being implemented in three overlapping phases. Phase I, consisting of 12 projects, is devoted primarily to roadbuilding and the development and improvement of potable water supplies, with its impact felt on major geographical and political subdivisions within the country. Phase II emphasizes school construction, water supply and distribution, with special emphasis being placed on public health and environmental sanitation activities. Phase III tackles the problems of population resettlement, improvement of agricultural methods and production, and long-range educational projects.

The projects selected for this program were based on these factors: (1) they must have a relatively high successful completion factor; (2) projects must be desirable to, and afford maximum participation by, the people; (3) projects must have an impact value against the Communist effort in Ecuador; and finally, (4) the projects must produce tangible evidence of United States support and interest in the people and the democratic government of Ecuador.

After approval of the program by the Ecuadorian government, the country team submitted it through the Unified Command and the Joint Staff to the Secretary of Defense. The Secretary of Defense approved the program for implementation on 8 May 1962.

With the Secretary of Defense's approval, implementation of the program has proceeded rapidly. To facilitate its implementation, a personnel augmentation of four U.S. officers and 29 enlisted technicians was requested and sent to Ecuador. The twelve projects of

Phase I took shape rapidly, with commencement dates ranging through October of 1962.

Three of the projects presently underway at Guayaquil, Loja, and Santa Rosa are described below.

At the port city of Guayaquil, a project has been initiated which provides tank trucks to haul potable water for the use of people in the crowded slum areas of the city, and the construction of ten 1600-gallon tanks dispersed at most convenient distribution points to receive, hold and distribute this water. This project is being supervised by one Ecuadorian Army officer and 10 enlisted men. Civilian manpower is used on the project. Work started on 13 August 1962. Construction materials and tanks have been delivered to several of the sites, and it is planned to have all tanks in place by the end of the year.

A second project in the vicinity of the interior village of Loja is the construction and repair of 22 kilometers of feeder road which will permit the people of the area to market their produce and will open up new areas for settlement. Two U.S. Army enlisted men have been assigned to this project as construction supervisors, working closely with Ecuadorian military personnel. Ecuadorian civilian labor, as well as mechanical equipment and handtools, have been made available on site. Seven 2½-ton dump trucks, one dozer, and one truck-mounted air compressor have been made available by the United States.

The Santa Rosa project consists of an open-type aqueduct, eleven kilometers in length, to provide water from a nearby river for irrigation of crop producing areas. Two U.S. Army enlisted men are presently assigned to this project as construction supervisors, working with one Ecuadorian project officer, 35 enlisted men, and civilian laborers.

The military civic action program for fiscal year 1963 envisions sending civic action mobile training teams to eleven Latin American, Middle Eastern, Far Eastern, and Tropical African countries. Active U.S. support is planned for 34 countries during this fiscal year. This support ranges from advice and assistance given by civic action mobile training teams to equipping engineer construction units.

115

It should be recognized that civic action is a many-sided program, ranging from the proper actions and attitudes of the individual soldier toward the people, to the performance of projects by military units. The necessity for a strong, well-directed, logical program with active and continuous support of the participating officials is a continuous challenge. Military civic action has untapped potential. The potential lies in the hearts and minds of the underprivileged who will benefit; in the unselfish desire to help others rise above squalor, poverty, and disease; in the superb know-how which inherently characterizes the U.S. soldier; and in the imagination and determination of those who plan for a peaceful advance of freedom.

AID'S Public Safety, Civic Action, and Community Development Programs

edited by RICHARD M. LEIGHTON
and RALPH SANDERS

The Agency for International Development (AID), successor to the International Cooperation Administration, was established in 1961 as an agency within the Department of State to emphasize long-range solutions to the problems of underdevelopment and instability as the "underprivileged" countries undergo modernization. Along with other government agencies, AID has been orienting its organization, plans, and programs to the more immediate problems of Communist subversion in the less-developed world. AID's concern is with any threat to the existence of a constituted government. Its

SOURCE: Chapter 12 of *New Dimensions in the Cold War*, edited by Richard M. Leighton and Ralph Sanders (Washington, D.C.: Industrial College of the Armed Forces, 1963). Adapted from material prepared by the Agency for International Development.

purview is not confined to active insurrection, but embraces also situations in which instability and the pressure of change have established an environment conducive to disorder and revolt. Underlying the Agency's efforts is the assumption that nations with self-sustaining economies and stable governments will have both the will and the strength to resist Communist pressures and subversion.

The AID Administrator holds a major responsibility in the direction of counterinsurgency. The Secretary of State has delegated to him the responsibility for review and coordination for all foreign assistance programs. In this role, he not only directs the economic aid programs of AID, but also insures that both the military and nonmilitary components of the U.S. foreign assistance programs conform to global aid and foreign policy guidance from the President and the Department of State. In addition to these responsibilities, the AID Administrator represents the Agency on the Special Group-Counterinsurgency constituted by the President in January 1962 to insure adequate programs, priority, and unity of effort in counterinsurgency.

Upon the AID Administrator rests the direct responsibility for carrying out the Agency's role in counterinsurgency. He has delegated this charge to the Deputy Administrator for Operations. A Special Assistant for Internal Defense, directly responsible to the Deputy Administrator, supervises the day-to-day matters of operation and coordination. At the Washington level AID officials work with representatives of other departments and agencies under the chairmanship of the State Department. Abroad the AID organization functions within the structure of the country team. Organization and authority have been delineated to permit synchronization of the entire range of AID programs with the needs of counterinsurgency.

Public Safety

AID has three counterinsurgency programs: a public safety program; a civic action program; and a community development program. The public safety program is not a new activity. The United States has aided the Philippine Constabulary for decades, the Iranian Gendarmerie since the end of the war, and the police of a number of nations under the technical assistance program during the fifties. Both CIA and DOD were involved in similar programs during this period. In 1954, at the direction of the NSC, the International Cooperation Administration assumed the major role in an increased effort to strengthen internal security forces throughout the free world. Applied to four countries in fiscal 1955, the program was extended to 21 countries in fiscal 1958 and to 38 countries in fiscal 1962. In the latter year the program cost approximately $15 million, was staffed with about 150 police advisors, and affected police forces totaling a million men.

The program seeks to increase the effectiveness of civil police organizations and their special forces in coping with riots and other forms of violence, conspiracy, and subversion, and to eliminate duplication and conflict between civil police and military forces. The President [Kennedy] has adopted a report on public safety worldwide, submitted by an Interdepartmental Committee on Police Programs created under the auspices of the Special Group-Counterinsurgency. This report establishes a new priority for police programs within the context of internal security and within the criteria employed in the country internal defense plan.

Current AID operations reflect the new emphasis on this program. In the absence of insurrection, the police are seen as the most sensitive point of contact between the government and the people. They are close to the focal points of unrest and are more acceptable than the military as keepers of order over long periods of time.

The Public Safety project in each country is unique in that it is geared to the country's stage of development, the competency of its civil police force, and other internal conditions. In some areas, only primitive notions of police science and service prevail, and improvement must start with fundamentals. In some former colonial states, the police forces lack experienced command personnel just as experienced managers are scarce in other fields. The forces must be staffed and reorganized and their policies adjusted to meet the changed emphasis and current needs. In other countries repressive military-type police forces must be converted into civil police forces oriented toward the public interest.

In still other areas, the changing economy has resulted in weakening tribal and family controls, thereby increasing police responsibilities and the need for improved law enforcement techniques. In like manner, where a country has a history of trained and disciplined police forces, there is still a need for greater efficiency and effectiveness in the use of modern concepts and procedures. Other problems, such as lack of equipment, illiteracy, inadequate personnel policies, including nepotism, insufficient funds, the increase of internal security responsibilities, and the absence of a tradition of police work as a public service—all combine to make the Public Safety Program more difficult to carry out.

The heart of the Public Safety Program is the training afforded police officers of the participating countries, for training at all levels is perhaps the greatest need of these nations. The AID provides this training within the host countries, in the United States, and in other countries where suitable facilities exist. At present there are some 165 experienced U.S. public safety technicians stationed in 26 countries at the request of the host governments to work with local public safety officials. To complement this effort, more than 1500 selected police officers from the participating countries have undergone training in the United States and returned to participate in their home training programs. In some instances, training of police officers is conducted in third countries to take advantage of monetary savings and similarities of language, culture, and police problems.

The AID also furnishes a minimum amount of essential civil police equipment to participating countries. This is primarily transportation, communication, and scientific equipment. In all cases this equipment is provided only after U.S. technicians carefully determine a country's need for this equipment and its ability to use it effectively. The AID encourages local governments and police forces to utilize their own resources for the purchase of equipment whenever possible.

Given the disorganized and rudimentary state of the public safety programs in many underdeveloped areas, AID contributions have been significant. In some areas, sizable improvements in police administration have been achieved. Elsewhere, the AID program has noticeably raised the level of police training. In still other areas, police communications and mobility have been strengthened and modernized. Traffic management, police public relations, and other special aspects of police work have also received attention. One of AID's most important contributions to the internal security of many underdeveloped countries has been in furnishing training for the effective control of riots and other civil disturbances.

The value of the AID Public Safety Program in combating insurgent movements in underdeveloped areas is thus of significant proportions. At relatively small expense to the United States, it helps to strengthen the nonmilitary defenses of the free world by promoting internal stability and respect for law and order in the ranks of the emerging nations.

Civic Action

The second counterinsurgency program, civic action, encourages the use of host country military forces and equipment on projects which contribute to social and economic development. The United States has supported such activities for nearly a decade where political considerations warranted it, as in the case of the Philippines and Korea. Policy directives and legislation since 1959 have given greater emphasis to this program. The primary aim is to improve the relations between the military and the civilian population. In many nations the military forces have engendered enmity by pursuing the preservation of their status and power at the expense of civilian needs. This is notably true in some Latin American countries. Where instability and latent insurgency stem from the failure of the governments to be responsive to the needs of the citizens, the military often pose a major obstacle to improved government-citizen rapport.

Civic action projects seek to facilitate an identification of governmental programs with the aspirations of the people. Various civic action projects are being carried out throughout the world. These include disaster relief and evacuation, medical services, medical evacuation from the rural areas, weather information, navigational aids, ship repair services, and community development projects. The construction of highways and feeder roads to link urban and rural areas is a major effort. This project is proving particularly successful in blending various objectives; it meets the people's "felt needs," increases military logistic capability, and promotes the market structure necessary for rapid economic growth. Civic action programs have assumed new significance and are supported by increased funding. New programs were installed in 12 countries in fiscal 1962, and were to be extended to 14 additional countries in the following years.

Community Development

The third counterinsurgency program under AID is community development. As the name suggests, the program contributes directly to the development of modern social institutions. Typically in the underdeveloped world the more traditionally oriented rural sector has been alienated from the more modern urban sector. As a result, the rural masses have been largely neglected. This is a particularly serious problem in Latin America where rural discontent has resulted in large migrations to the urban areas. There the peasants find not the increased standards of living that they desire, but a situation of severe unemployment. The result has been a rapid growth of the most stark slums and the emergence of a volatile political element readily susceptible to insurgency.

The community development program seeks to establish the two-way channels of communication and responsibility between the rural sector and the government. It acts through self-help programs to elicit from the villagers an appreciation of social and economic development efforts, to foster in them a political allegiance to the government, and create self-sustaining communities with a sense of political and social responsibility. This approach recognizes that the minds of men are the ultimate and decisive targets of the protagonists of insurgency. It acknowledges that society itself is at war, and that the resources, motives, and targets of this struggle are found almost wholly within the local population.

Community development projects vary widely in character. The projects themselves are less important than the spirit in which they are carried out. The essence of the program is that it is "with the people," not "for the people." The successful village-level worker never arrives at the village with a predetermined plan, but rather puts upon the village leadership the responsibility for choosing the projects and arranging for the use of the village resources. The host government, in conjunction with the U.S. AID mission, provides the resources that the people themselves cannot supply. In this way the people in the existing or newly created villages have a sense of full participation in the modernization process.

AID has initiated a rather unique community development effort in Southeast Asia. Labelled the "Strategic Hamlet" program, it is applied to villages in the throes of active guerrilla operations. The guerrillas have used both propaganda and terror to obtain from the people the food, supplies, and information that they need. The Strategic Hamlet is a village which has been equipped to prevent this exploitation as well as to further the economic development of the population. The DOD and AID share the funding of "village packages" which include such items as agricultural implements, medical supplies, pyrotechnic pistols and other small arms, fence posts, barbed wire, and village alarm systems. In addition, AID is providing radios and transceivers to the villagers. Along with the other AID counterinsurgency operations, this program is expected to have an important bearing on the course of events in South Vietnam.

Conclusion

The AID counterinsurgency programs are faced with a challenge that is genuinely awesome and with problems of extreme complexity. The Agency will continue to have to make decisions between long range goals and short range considerations, always bearing in mind that while the problems are old, the planning emphasis and funding priorities have changed radically. On the basis of the record so far, there is room for cautious optimism.

5 The Politics of the Developing Nations

Crucial to the developmental process in any underdeveloped state is the political process. Modernization above all requires social engineering of a high order. The often conflicting forces within a society must be understood and brought into accord with the aims of a modern state. This task is primarily political because it requires the consent, whenever feasible, of the people of the traditional society. There are two basic manifestations of this political process in the less developed countries: (1) the roles played by the various elites in the society and (2) the utility of the political party.

The first of these manifestations is understandably the most important in the early stages of a nation's political development. In fact, the experience of some underdeveloped countries suggests that the success of the modernization process requires that modern values be fully assimilated by as large a leadership group as possible and that this elite be capable of effective action. In order to share its purposes with the people, the elite must act within the context of a mass movement, which it must organize. The mass movement may then serve as the embryo of the modern national community it is to forge.

In the long run, equally important in the developmental process is the emergence of an institutionalized means of political expression —the political party. Most less developed nations have carried over from their colonial heritage some variant of this institution. It is most important to observe the roles which these various institutions play in their respective societies. Particularly significant is the high incidence of a lack of party competition in these states. Furthermore, there is an expectedly high incidence of political instability in those countries which lack party competition. This selection raises some of the theoretical aspects of developing viable political processes in the less developed nations of the world.

Building the Newest Nations: Short-run Strategies and Long-run Problems

by WILLIAM J. FOLTZ

Building a nation is an exceedingly difficult and long task. Whether or not one accepts Professor Strayer's prediction of "an endless round of coups, conquests, revolutions, and wars," it is evident that the so-called "new nations" that have gained independence since World War II have only begun the arduous path to achieving viable and stable national existence. Indeed, as Professor Scott has shown, more than a century of independent existence has not sufficed to give the people of Latin America fully meaningful national identities. Professor Friedrich's suggestion that an integrated national identity may be too ambitious a goal for the new nations emphasizes, as do the leaders of these countries themselves, that their immediate task is the establishment of a strong governmental apparatus able to serve and control the population. The old argument over the priority of state or nation is being resolved by these countries' leaders in favor of first building the state as an instrument to bring about the nation.

As Professor Merritt's study of the American experience shows, however, obtaining even the sort of cooperation necessary for the regular functioning of a state apparatus may be dependent on the prior establishment of a strong sense of common identity and a com-

SOURCE: Reprinted by permission from *Nation-Building*, edited by Karl W. Deutsch and William J. Foltz (New York: Atherton Press, 1963).

mon outlook among the "politically relevant strata" of a society on a wide variety of issues. A glance around today's globe suffices to show, however, that in many new states forceful governmental structures have been established that do not approach the level of internal communication and mutual comprehension of the thirteen American colonies on the eve of the Revolution. The problem here, it seems to me, is the composition and extent of the "politically relevant strata." A large proportion of the eighteenth-century American population not only possessed the skills requisite for participation in political decision-making, but also energetically insisted on such participation. Few rural hamlets were so small or isolated that they did not contain one voice whose words had to be reckoned with at some distant center of government. In contrast, most of the nations that have achieved their independence since World War II have had what is, from a short-range point of view at least, the good fortune to possess a narrowly constricted and homogeneous set of politically relevant strata. Furthermore, the large gap separating these people from the masses has permitted them to maintain themselves as a stable and nearly self-sufficient political elite during the most trying periods of political transition.

In most cases, this is not a gap of inherited traditional status, but one of modern achievement, most significantly educational achievement.[1] This, if anything, makes the gap more permanent, for ascribed status distinctions can sometimes be abolished overnight for political purposes, but most of the population cannot be taught overnight, or even in a few generations, the skills necessary to participate meaningfully and effectively in politics. The gap is between those living in the modern world and participating in the crucial decisions of the political arena and those living essentially as did their ancestors, bereft not only of skills for modern politics and other modern occupations, but, in some cases, of even a minimal sense of identity with political structures and the people animating them. Although this gap provides the greatest long-run challenge to those who would build an integrated nation, in the short run it has given

[1] For a similar educational distinction of elite from mass, see Claude Tardits, *Porto Novo* (Paris: Mouton, 1958,) p. 11.

the elite the great flexibility of maneuver that is necessary to seize and consolidate the power of the state.

The educational structures of the newest states tend to reinforce polarization between elite and mass. Typically, there exists a great mass of people with no or only primary education and then, at the other extreme, a small but significant number of people with university-level training. What is lacking are people educated to the intermediate high school and junior high levels that characterize the bulk of the population in most advanced societies.[2] The reason for this gap is, on the surface, a good one. Because of the lack of educational funds, students for postprimary education must be rigorously selected at the sixth grade level. Those that succeed are then pushed to the limit of their abilities, which may be very great indeed. Without a large intermediate sector of reasonably competent and educated mid-elites, however, complex issues of government and administration are not interpreted and transmitted throughout society in meaningful terms that the masses can easily grasp. At the top, issues are faced in all their complexity; at the bottom, they are grouped and boiled down to simple slogans—"Independence now!" "One man, one vote!" Issues cannot be meaningfully debated within the populace at large, and votes tend to become mere approving plebiscites.

If, in society as a whole, there are few individuals in everyday life prepared to interpret and relate the problems of the elite to the masses, there are also few institutions capable of bridging the gap. In most African, and some Asian countries, the single, mass political party (*parti unique*) has played this role and has been the primary means of bringing the masses into contact with the political culture and inducting individuals into political roles.[3] Where the politi-

[2] In Ghana, for instance, only about 12 percent of those finishing primary school are admitted to advanced secondary training. Similarly, in the Ivory Coast in 1957 "only 750 out of 5,739 who completed primary school continued their education." At least half of these then went on to university training. Both countries have recently taken steps to expand secondary education. See Ruth Sloan Associates, *The Educated African* (New York: Praeger, 1962), esp. pp. 334–340, 460–469.

[3] The *parti unique* is both an elite and a link. . . . The *parti unique* has as a goal to forge new elites, to create a new governing class, to unite and

126

cal party apparatus has been strong and active, the greatest political acculturation of the masses has taken place, as a comparison of, say, Guinea with Upper Volta or Ghana with Sierra Leone would show. However, the limits of this political acculturation should be noted. The masses are, for the most part, still associated with the receiving end of the political order. As Professor Scott put it, they are still "subjects," and their participation is ideally limited to applause on cue and, at most, to sullen foot-dragging when changes appear to be for the worse. Since the single, mass political parties, more than formal governmental or purely social organizations, often seem to be the prime mediators between elite and mass, they may, as Professor Emerson suggests, hold out the best hope for building the newest nations. We shall, therefore, take a more thorough look at their past successes and future possibilities.

Most of the currently ruling political parties in the newest states grew up under the late colonial regimes as instruments for attaining national independence. Particularly in the British and French colonial empires, the single, mass parties were singularly successful in leading the way to independence and quickly consolidating control over the government and administrative apparatuses once independence was achieved. The strength and success of these parties have rested on four principal factors. First, in "Independence!" they had a rallying cry of universal appeal. Typically, in any competitive party situation, the party that first proclaimed, "Freedom now," "Uhuru," or "N'dépendence" ended up on top once it had made itself the recognized spokesman for the feelings of vague revolt and common identity that usually make up modern nationalism in the underdeveloped countries. Its espousal of national independence provided a focus around which both elite and mass could unite. Second, the single, mass party usually included virtually all the modern elite. These men were united by ties of personal friendship, frequently reinforced by common educational and agitational ex-

---

train political leaders capable of organizing the country, for the masses cannot govern themselves. . . . The party establishes a direct and permanent contact between [the political elite] and the country." Maurice Duverger, *Les Partis politiques* (Paris: Armand Colin, 1958), p. 288.

periences and by dedication to the nationalist cause. Those members of the modern elite who did not join the mass party initially were generally co-opted at a later date or were so compromised by association with the colonial administration that they were ineffective as opposition leaders. Third, because of the dominance of the nationalist issue and because of the general lack of other modern structures, the single political party had no serious competition from other modern associations as a focus for popular loyalties. Finally, the single, mass party was generally well organized. The conditions of the political struggle and the dedication of the top elite to the party as the prime instrument of political change led the elite to give the major portion of their energies and resources to building a solid, responsive organization capable of disciplined action in response to directives from the top and able to ferret out and exploit feelings of dissatisfaction among the masses for political ends. The mass party became the framework within which ethnic, caste, and regional differences among the population at large could be submerged in the search for a common goal. It both embodied and promoted a preliminary sense of national unity and identity.

But winning independence, although it may be a necessary condition, is only the first and perhaps easiest step in building a nation. The new state apparatus must then be solidly implanted and extended, and the loyalty of the people to a stable governing regime, not to an agitational opposition movement, must be assured. However, the very factors making the mass party such an effective tool in the struggle for independence and permitting it to take over governmental power may be weakened by the day-to-day exercise of governmental responsibilities and by the nation-building process itself. Once formal independence is won, the unifying slogan of "Independence" has lost its magic force, and it is unlikely that anything quite so dramatic and effective can be found to replace it. Defending a revolution is always a less exciting and more onerous task than making it. Frequently, newly independent states seize on a new derivative slogan or goal to replace "independence" as a means of unifying both elite and mass. These secondary goals have frequently involved transforming the world outside the state to bring it more into line with the desires and presumed advantages of the new state, thus symbolically continuing the movement of independence. Such movements have sometimes, but not always, sought to export a national revolution or, as in Africa recently, to continue the independence movement to areas not yet favored by an enlightened colonial master. Of the same sort are the many irredentist movements designed to annex a lost or related territory or region, as for example, the recent disputes between Morocco and Mauritania or Ghana and Togo. With such direct extensions of the goal of "national independence," governments frequently may promote a regional or federal unity movement of some sort, which may seek to reactivate popular emotions by redirecting them toward a greater whole. Pan-Africanism and Pan-Arabism are well-known examples.

Although turning to the outside world may provoke as strong an emotional yearning for unity as did the simpler search for national political unity and independence formerly, it may, in the short run, simply dilute or confuse more specific national sentiment. To the degree that it makes the success of the territorial nationalist movement dependent on that of a greater whole, it may in the long run succeed only in calling into question the worth of the national regime when the larger unity proves unrealizable.

The new state may try to unite its people by focusing animosities and frustrations on some external enemy, just as the nationalist movement focused its resentments on the colonial power or previous ruling class. To this end, the term "neocolonialism" has recently been invented. Those who brandish "neocolonialism" as a political slogan warn against continued domination by the former masters, now presumably operating behind the scenes through control of indigenous puppets and the new state's economy. Moise Tshombe's regime in Katanga is generally presented as the most blatant example of neocolonialism, but domestic difficulties in the most anti-imperialist states may be blamed on secret neocolonists. "Neocolonialism" as a political slogan does have the great advantage of being almost universally applicable. By definition, neocolonialism operates behind the scenes, so virtually anything can be blamed on it. At the same time, however, its very ethereality means that neocolonialism is not directly experienced by the man in the street as was foreign political or military control, and it may, thereby, be a less effective political slogan.

Finally, the new state may choose some purely internal, non-symbolic goal to replace national independence as a national rallying cry. The "battle for economic development" is the most common and significant such goal today, as one would expect. However praise-worthy economic development may be as a national goal and how-ever important it may be for long-term nation-building, it is still not likely to have the political potency of "independence." No matter how it is explained to them, few people are likely to make volun-tarily and happily the sacrifices required in order to increase the gross national product by 3 per cent per annum or whatever else the goal might be. Furthermore, to the extent that most of the new states are primarily agricultural countries, the new regimes are obliged to earn precious domestic developmental capital from the sweat of peasantry fulfilling and overfulfilling their quotas. Thus, the first results of the drive for economic development may be a tougher lot for the very people for whom the new regime was brought into power—a fact which is unlikely to increase the masses' esteem for the regime.

As the mass party in the newly independent state is deprived of "independence" as a national rallying cry, so, too, its organiza-tion may suffer once it has passed from systematic opposition to coping with the demands of day-to-day administration. Talents that once were available for the crucial work of party organization may now be preoccupied with running a ministry or government bureau. This will be particularly true where the conditions under which independence was obtained led to the withdrawal of European ad-visors and technicians and threw the whole technical and adminis-trative burden on the shoulders of the young indigenous politicians. Unless new sources of loyal organizational and administrative tal-ents can be found immediately, the party's organization—and, there-fore, the major link between the regime and the masses—is likely to be weakened.

If, in the days of nationalist agitation for independence, the mass party provided the unique and inclusive instrument for popular political participation, this is not likely to be the case after independence is attained. Governing an independent country requires indigenous participation in a great variety of new, formally constituted units. A civil service and national army are only the minimal, though most essential, organizations that must be staffed. Although these, like the governmental apparatus, will formally be brought under the control of the mass party, they can be expected to become new focuses of loyalty and to develop new goals, priorities, and methods that are at variance with those of the mass party. With increased specialization of function, the elite will share fewer and fewer common perspectives and experiences and will develop personal and group interests that could well produce internal scissions that were absent when the mass political party was the single organ of political expression, participation, and planning.

Of course, in theory the new organizations should complement the mass party as the means of bridging the gap between the elite and the masses. However, if a struggle for influence pitting army or administration against the party develops, the very contacts of the new organizations with the masses may serve to divide the people more deeply than they were when only the party undertook to link them with the realm of modern politics. This will be particularly the case in cultures where personal leadership is important, and an army general, top administrator, or cabinet minister may build a personal following among the population at large.

The dispersion of leadership talents and the competition of different decision-making units may be further accentuated if economic development is given top priority by the ruling elite. It is in part to prevent the creation of autonomous domestic decision-making units with a basis of economic power that many new states have refused to expand the private sector of the economy, even when such expansion would clearly contribute to economic development. It is not, in this sense, paradoxical that one of the most "revolutionary" new states, Guinea, should have tried repressing all domestic free enterprise while signing major contracts for exploitation of her natural resources with a consortium of Western private concerns. As the Guineans saw it, the foreigners would remain outside the sphere of domestic politics, but any Guinean private enterprise might augment fissiparous tendencies in the body politic. Elsewhere in the new states, governments have promoted or insisted upon partnership with private capital in all major economic enterprises to ensure the regime's control over the decisions and credit for any success.

Even where economic planning and execution remain firmly in governmental hands, however, one may expect to find a new center of power created in the planning ministry, allied or not allied with the civil service against the party and regime. This would seem almost inevitable if economic development is to be given serious priority. On almost every level, the demands of economic efficiency are sure to conflict at some point with the demands of political expediency or orthodoxy. Since their independence, Indonesia and Ghana have continually faced such conflicts. This type of conflict was illustrated most dramatically in December, 1962, when the Senegalese party leaders felt obliged to remove the prime minister and dismantle the planning and administrative apparatus under his control when they seemed to threaten party primacy.

But this is a realm in which the single-party regime must tread lightly, for the outcome of the struggle for pre-eminence is not at all foreordained. The further development has gone, the more opposition the regime will arouse among the technically oriented younger elites if the party chooses to slow down or stop change as a means of maintaining political control. This has, of course, been particularly the case in Burma, Pakistan, and Sudan, where technical military elites have seized power from the politicians. As Professor Wilson points out in his chapter, the military may have its own way of building a nation with or without the participation of a party apparatus.

In a somewhat broader perspective, the implementation of rapid economic and social change and, in particular, of educational development can open a whole range of new problems centered around controlling the burgeoning new elites. In part this is simply a qualitative problem. The promising young men who are trained after independence has been won will have quite different associations, perceptions, and preoccupations from those of their elders of the nationalist generation. Furthermore, since the nationalist generation is likely to come into power around age forty at the most, it is unlikely to fade from the scene so quickly as the new generation would like. On the other hand, the new generation is likely to have more formal education than its elders, particularly in technical domains. Also, since it will in all probability be trained abroad for the most part, it will escape the direct influence of the single-party regime during the crucial formative years of adolescence. It is not surprising that a recent survey of African students in France revealed that 63 per cent considered themselves in serious conflict with their governments.[4] After their return to home, one would naturally expect these young men to side with one of the alternative loci of power in the country, particularly if they are blocked, as they must be if the single-party regime's continuity is to be maintained, in their attempt to accede immediately to posts of high responsibility and power. This clash of interests was emphasized in Guinea in 1962, when several of the young intellectuals sought to impose their political vision on the single-party regime. In a direct confrontation, the party leaders jailed the intellectual leaders, recalled Guinean students from abroad, locked rebellious *lycée* students in their school, sent in the loyal party youth group, made up of the educationally underprivileged, to teach the students a lesson—something they did with considerable gusto. In this state, as in other new states, the regime has, in times of stress, tended to fall back on loyal, if uneducated, political cadres rather than on the new elites. Although this may be a proper response to a short-run problem, it may have adverse effects on long-run political development.

But the rapid creation of new elites has a quantitative dimension of equal importance. It is one thing to integrate smoothly ten, twenty, or fifty returning students a year into the single-party regime and to inculcate in them the established political values and per-

[4] J. P. N'Diaye, *Enquête sur les étudiants noirs en France* (Paris: Réalités Africaines, 1962), p. 223.

ceptions, but it is quite another to integrate a hundred or five hundred, particularly if they cannot be given the positions of top leadership to which they aspire because their fathers or older brothers are reluctant to step down. Without the clear necessity of pulling together to achieve independence and with a wider range of choices than faced the nationalist generation, these young men are unlikely to melt quietly into the previously established single-party regime. Nor are they so likely as were their elders to make the attempt to bridge the gap separating them from the masses, since by doing so they may only diminish the distinctiveness of their personal elite position without necessarily gaining corresponding political advantage. With no provisions for a loyal open opposition, a disloyal covert opposition may seem the only choice.

The emphasis on rapid social and economic change also poses problems for the single-party state on the level of the masses. If, through economic and social planning, one increases the rate of popular mobilization,[5] one also increases the demands made on the government. Although this mobilization is essential for building national sentiment among the masses, it may also threaten the regime if the government cannot keep pace with the new demands. Although in most cases this social mobilization was begun under the colonial regime, the colonial power was seldom attentive to these demands, even if it had been capable of responding. The nationalist single-party movement learned to be attentive to the masses' demands and used the colonial regime's reluctance to respond as an argument for seizing power. The independent single-party regime may continue to be attentive, but it is unlikely to possess the resources for responding effectively if mobilization proceeds at too great a pace. Alternatively, it may emphasize building an effective response capability by giving the younger technical elites their head and playing down the political party structure. But, in doing this, it may end by making the new regime less well attuned to the immediate wants of the mobilized and dissatisfied masses, thereby inad-

[5] On the concept of mobilization, see Karl W. Deutsch, "Social Mobilization and Political Development," *American Political Review*, LV, No. 3 (1961), 493–514.

vertently re-creating a situation analogous to that of the colonial era. A rigid new bureaucracy, even if technically competent and filled with good intentions, may open the possibility of new popular revolts led, perhaps, by disaffected politicians of the older nationalist generation who have maintained their links with the masses. Such a conflict between a distant technical bureaucracy and politicians of the nationalist generation has been particularly acute in the new states where the military has seized power.[6]

The new states will increasingly be obliged to make some hard long-range decisions for which the experience and habits acquired in the period of nationalist agitation will provide little guidance. Stated most baldly, the polar choices open to the new states hold terrors equal to those of Scylla and Charybdis. At one extreme, a state may choose to ride the tiger of exacerbated pluralism and possible internal strife and disintegration, and, at the other extreme, it may choose to restrain social and economic change to a level that can be handled by the existing political structures. Similarly, the new regimes face a choice between transforming themselves completely to the profit of the new postnationalist elites, with the attendant danger of losing political attentiveness to popular demands and what remains of the prestige (and personnel) of the nationalist movement, and, on the other hand, constricting access to the political elite, with the possibilities of political stagnation and turning the younger generation of elites against the regime.

It is difficult to predict at what point a given regime will succeed in striking a balance between these extremes. In general, it would seem that the closer to either extreme a regime comes, the poorer its chance of maintaining political integrity and eventually building a nation. Long-run pressures, especially those of an economic sort, would seem to be on the side of a more pluralist political process permitting entry of at least some new elites into the legitimate political arena and associating at least some newly mobilized sectors of the population with these elites through structures more or

[6] See Lucian W. Pye, "The Army in Burmese Politics," in John J. Johnson, ed., *The Role of the Military in Underdeveloped Countries* (Princeton: Princeton University Press, 1962), pp. 231–251.

less outside the existing single-party framework. If this increase in political and social pluralism does not seriously weaken central governmental authority and create focuses of loyalty that challenge the legitimacy of the nation itself, rather than just a particular group of leaders or a specific policy, the nation-building process should be considerably advanced. For such a dynamic compromise to be maintained over the long run, the existing regime in most of the newest states must first feel itself secure enough from disruptive internal and external pressures to permit it to accept the necessary loosening of direct political control. At least in the short run, most such regimes will require absolute loyalty from new elites and acquiescence from the population at large, if only as evidence that the state is firmly enough established to permit the nation to be built.

Ensuring the short-run stability of the new states has led many regimes into practices which appear particularly objectionable to most people with a liberal democratic tradition. The "cult of personality" built around the national hero, the mouthing of seemingly senseless revolutionary slogans after the apparent revolution has been won, and the suppression of opposition groups and leaders are among the practices most commonly noted in the Western press. Although the disadvantages of these practices are readily apparent—at least to the outside observer with no immediate policy responsibilities—they may also serve useful functions in permitting the regimes to survive the initial period of building the state and make a successful transition to building a nation. Popular identification with a national hero and commitment to a revolutionary program, whether or not confined purely to the verbal level, both have the advantage of dissociating the state from a particular group of individuals making up the nationalist regime and permitting the people at large or new elites to serve and identify with a specific leader or set of policies. The national hero can retain not only the loyalty of the mass of the people, who are perhaps annoyed at specific governmental agents for specific causes, but can also go against his own lieutenants and bring new elites into the regime. Both Nasser and Nkrumah have used their positions in this way. Similarly, concentration on some sort of ideology, even if only symbolic, permits popular recognition of particular governmental functions above and beyond the specific individuals fulfilling those functions. At the same time, it holds up a national goal for younger elites to follow, and, by their acceptance of such a goal, they may more easily be brought into smoothly-functioning relationships with the incumbent elite.

Finally, the suppression of opposition leaders, and even of some of the new elites, may, with luck, permit the new states to get over the most trying period of postrevolutionary letdown without a collapse of the ruling regime, either through internal bickering or outside attacks. To the extent that the new state concentrates on building a more continuous educational system at home and to the extent that it has time to indoctrinate the younger elites in loyalty to the new political order, succeeding elites should pose fewer problems to the regime than does the immediate postrevolutionary generation.

The ability of the newest states to grow out of their initial periods of restrictive consolidation of power and into a more balanced society-wide pattern of national growth will depend in part on the willingness of the leaders to envisage fundamental revisions in the relations between the regime and its people and also on whether the adoption of less restrictive policies brings with it sufficient rewards to make the risk of pluralism worth taking. Certainly, if economic and social development seem impossible no matter what course of action is adopted or if the nations in the best position to assist a new state turn a deaf ear to a regime's initial pleas for assistance, the sterile pattern of repression, stagnation, and revolt will become the lot of most states. Instead of profiting from the West's arduous history of nation-building, the newest nations may then be condemned to repeat the long apprenticeship of "coups, conquests, revolutions, and wars" before they, too, evolve viable national societies.

Comparative Case Studies

Algeria

Algeria is located on the North African shore of the Mediterranean and is bounded on the east by Tunisia, on the west by Morocco, and on the south by the Sahara. Its vast land area covers 852,000 square miles, 125,000 of which constitute Algeria proper, while the remainder consists of the sparsely inhabited Saharan territories. Understandably the nation's climate varies from the moist and temperate near the Mediterranean to the hot and arid of the Sahara. Its soils are not outstandingly fertile, but are sufficiently so in the coastal belt to sustain a prosperous agriculture.

It is estimated that the current (1965) population of Algeria is slightly in excess of ten million people. In addition, more than 500,000 Algerian nationals live and work in France. The vast majority of the Algerian people are ethnically Arab, but there is a large Berber minority of approximately one million, concentrated mainly in the Kabyle Mountains of northeastern Algeria. Prior to independence in 1962, more than a million of Algeria's inhabitants were of European stock—French, Spanish, Maltese, and Jewish. Now less than 50,000 ethnic Europeans remain in the country.

In 1961 Algerian income per capita reached a high of $281, but this figure is extremely deceptive since it, of course, includes both the European and Europeanized Moslem incomes as well as the nominal incomes of the Saharan nomads. Now the income per capita has slumped to the more realistic level of less than $100, with a further decline probable because of stagnant economic conditions. Illiteracy averages about 80 per cent, although at present approximately 30 per cent of Algerian school-age children are in school. The social structure of the nation varies greatly in quality from the French-educated intellectual and professional classes in the cities to the great masses of tradition-bound rural peasants.

The Challenge and the Strategy

A society which has been so greatly revolutionized demands that revolutionary solutions be devised to meet its problems. It will insist that a way be found to mobilize these masses who have been freed from the traditional disciplines and thrown into a drastic, disillusioned world by holding up before them a collective ideal, the building of a harmonious economy capable of assuring employment and a decent standard of living for all.[1]

On July 1, 1962, Algeria received its independence following 132 years of French colonial rule. The Algerian nation had just undergone what was undoubtedly the most violent anticolonial revolution in this generation. It had lasted eight years, desolated much of the rural Algerian hinterland, and reduced the national population by approximately 20 per cent. The problems facing the new state are formidable: the creation of a sense of national identity, the development of viable political institutions, and the continuation of economic modernization started under French auspices.

The Algerian leadership, similar to that of most of the world's newly independent, less developed nations, confronts simultaneously what Gabriel Almond has described as the "four problems of democratic nation building."[2] First, it has to create Algerians out of all the ethnic and religious groups which inhabit contemporary Algeria. Second, it has to create a framework of bureaucratic authority and habits of obedience to government in simple and illiterate villagers, who form the overwhelming majority of the population. It has to create citizen-participants out of this same human material, giving them the right to vote before they can read, before they properly know what government is. And as it strives to raise the level of literacy and acquaint its people with the amenities and physical goods of modern civilization, it must somehow respond to the growing demands for physical goods and welfare. It confronts a national

[1] Pierre Bourdieu, *The Algerians,* in English translation by Alan C. M. Ross (Boston: Beacon, 1962), pp. 191–92.

[2] Gabriel A. Almond, "Democracy and the New Nations," *Stanford Today* (Autumn, 1964).

revolution, an authority revolution, a participation revolution, and a welfare revolution all at one time.

Obviously the leadership cannot yield in all four directions at once. It "must give a higher priority to the creation of a nation and of effective government authority before giving way to demands for participation and welfare. Indeed we may say that it must first create a nation and effective government authority if it is ever going to be able to respond to demands for political participation and welfare."[3]

Broadly speaking there appear to have been at least two basic patterns of modernization from which Algeria could have chosen, given the complexity and scope of the problems involved. One possible alternative would have been the approach chosen by President Habib Bourguiba in neighboring Tunisia. In essence, Bourguibism "combines an intransigence upon the principles with flexibility in the choice of means to implement them."[4] It is more properly a set of tactics rather than an ideology, a pragmatic, socially oriented type of nationalism rather than a variant of Marxism.

The other choice that Algeria might have made is "Sukarnoism," a militantly nationalistic, anticolonialist approach such as that espoused by Indonesia's President Sukarno. The essence of this approach is to place great emphasis on symbols and slogans such as "guided democracy" and to take an ideological approach to all major questions of domestic or foreign policy.

In between these alternatives rest several variations on the main themes, depending in content upon both the characteristics of the particular leader and the external circumstances in which he finds himself and his country. Premier Fidel Castro of Cuba tends to resemble the Sukarno image. President Gamal Abdel Nasser of Egypt, on the other hand, tends to project a more moderate, pragmatic image despite occasional emotional outbursts.

Algeria under the recently deposed President Ahmed Ben Bella

[3] Ibid.

[4] Charles A. Micaud, *Tunisia: The Politics of Modernization* (New York: Praeger, 1964), p. 77.

seemed to have opted for the Sukarno solution—an approach which emphasizes ideology rather than pragmatism, slogans rather than compromises, foreign policy rather than domestic development, charismatic leadership rather than mass political organizations. In short, Algeria seemed to have chosen the politics of charisma. Under the new regime this approach will probably be changed significantly.

The First Priority: An Algerian Nation

The problem of creating a sense of national identity in Algeria is surprisingly difficult. Unlike neighboring Tunisia and Morocco, Algeria had never experienced any genuine existence as a definable national entity antedating French colonial rule. Turkish rule had never taken hold in the country and was nominal in character. During the long tenure of the French any expression of a nascent Algerian national consciousness was ruthlessly suppressed. Sporadic revolts occurred in the Kabylia Mountains until 1871, when Algeria was finally considered "pacified." Tribal property was seized, and tribal authority and cohesion were destroyed. The French policy of limited assimilation tended to siphon off most of the would-be nationalist leadership. As late as 1936 Ferhat Abbas, former president of the Algerian National Assembly, stated in an oft-cited comment: "I will not die for the Algerian fatherland, for this fatherland does not exist. I have not encountered it. I have questioned history. I have questioned the quick and the dead. I have visited cemeteries. No one has spoken to me of such a thing—you cannot build on wind." [5]

Algeria, when it received its independence, was in the unenviable position of having to create its own personality and national institutions out of the chaos of a revolution. What was to be done with the French settlers, the *pieds noirs,* who were first-, second-, third-, and even fourth-generation "Algerians"? To a great extent the settler minority eliminated itself, first by waging a vicious, bloody, but unsuccessful counterguerrilla war and then, having

[5] Michael K. Clark, *Algeria in Turmoil* (New York: Praeger, 1959), p. 17.

failed, by departing in great numbers. Those French *colons* who remained were then given the option of becoming Algerian citizens, but it was made clear that this type of citizenship was second-class. Despite the obvious advantages of retaining European skills and European participation in the life of the country, the concept of Algerian national identity took precedence over more pragmatic considerations. The creation of a "genuine" Algerian nation was further enhanced by the sweeping three-stage wave of nationalization of settler property. Between October 1962 and September 1963 the Algerian government, both reacting to and accelerating the departure of all Europeans, sequestered all foreign-owned land.

What could be done with the ruggedly independent Berber minority located primarily in the Grand Kabylia? Already two abortive uprisings have occurred in this area, one in the autumn of 1963 and the second in the fall of 1964. Both failed, and the leader of the Kabyle rebels, Hoçine Ait Ahmed, has been captured and imprisoned. Rebel resistance in this area still smolders, although it appears to be disintegrating rapidly. Still another abortive uprising against the government took place in the early summer of 1964 in the Aures Mountains on the fringes of the Sahara in eastern Algeria. The leader of this group, Colonel Mohammed Chaabani, a dissident guerrilla fighter, was captured and executed in September 1964. The Arab Moslem majority has now, on the surface at least, achieved a genuine and effective sense of national unity.

The third major aspect of the deposed leadership's campaign to create an Algerian national identity is evidenced in the field of foreign policy. Not yet three years old, Algeria was playing a grandstand role in international relations. In Africa, Algeria had placed itself in the forefront of an anticolonialist crusade. President Ben Bella had become a major leader in the Organization of African Unity. Algiers itself had become a haven and major staging area for hundreds of Portuguese exiles, mainly from the Portuguese colonies of Angola, Mozambique, and Portuguese Guinea. It was in Algiers that the militant anticolonialist periodical *Révolution Africaine* was published. In the fall of 1964 Algeria took a very active stand on behalf of the Congolese rebels. At that time Ben Bella not only condemned the air drops of Belgian paratroops but also pledged arms and volunteers to aid the rebels.

In Middle Eastern affairs the now deposed Ben Bella was chosen by the Arab League to present its case against Israel before the United Nations. It was he who attempted to pressure Prince Faisal of Saudi Arabia into dropping that nation's opposition to the revolutionary republican regime in Yemen. Operating on a wider scale, Ben Bella on several occasions had urged the United States to open talks with Cuba, hoping apparently to pave the way for American acceptance of Castro.

Perhaps most significant of all in this connection, Algeria was scheduled to play host to the so-called "Second Bandung" Conference of Afro-Asian nations in late June 1965. For this purpose the Algerian government constructed, with Egyptian assistance, a huge new hotel–conference hall twenty-three stories high. After the coup on June 19, 1965, the conference was postponed until November 5 at the instigation of most of the nations scheduled to participate. Communist China dissented until the last.

Another important aspect of Algeria's efforts at nation-building may be found in its attempt to create a "new" and individual ideology. Algeria is officially described as a popular and democratic republic, but in practice it pursued what President Ben Bella labeled a "specifically Algerian Socialism." As he explained it on one occasion, "I am neither a Marxist nor an anti-Marxist, but I realize what our liberation owed to Marxist ideas."[6] Actually this Algerian ideology appeared to be a pragmatic accommodation of the doctrines of Mohammed with the doctrines of Marx. Intellectual Algerians thought of themselves as forming a doctrinal bridge between the Arab world and the Communist world, while at the same time retaining an umbilical relationship, both culturally and economically, with France. This ideology may now be significantly modified in the direction of traditional Islamic doctrine.

What was this "Algerian Socialism" in practice? While Algeria was not a Communist state, it was obviously far to the left of

[6] *The Nation,* November 23, 1963, p. 342.

American and West European democracies. There were no legal opposition parties in Algeria. All political parties except the National Liberation Front (FLN) had been outlawed. This ban included the Algerian Communist party. Ben Bella had said: "There is no place in Algeria for an opposition. Every Algerian has the right to criticize me, but the place for that is in the party itself."[7]

The Algerian government had secured for itself a monopoly of all communications media. The radio in Algeria during the French colonial period was already state-owned. The three remaining French-language newspapers were seized by the government in September 1963. One newspaper plant was used to produce *Le Peuple*, the party organ of the FLN. This publication has now been replaced with a new official daily, *El Moujahid*. Algeria had also embarked upon a radical land reform program embracing not only land abandoned by the departing French *colons* but also land owned by native Algerians in excess of 125 acres. At the same time the Algerian government had undertaken a sweeping program of nationalization of industries, mines, banks, and private businesses of all types.

What kind of "nation-building" pattern emerged from this variegated picture? On the affirmative side one saw a shrewd, charismatic leader overcoming internal opposition and suppressing or eliminating troublesome dissident minorities, while creating the proud image of a major anticolonialist power pursuing its own indigenous brand of socialism. On the negative side one saw a one-party authoritarian state tending toward totalitarianism. One saw foreign policy issues used to divert and distract the attention of the Algerian people from the urgent domestic problems confronting the nation. While in the short run a leadership role in the continuing anticolonialist crusade may have been satisfying to the ego of a newly independent state like Algeria, it seemed only to have postponed a day of internal reckoning, to have frittered away precious resources of materials, time, and talent which could better have been employed at home.

Moreover this attempt to play a "bridging role" between the

[7] *The Reporter,* October 10, 1963, p. 35.

147

Arab and the Communist worlds, this eclectic doctrinal approach, may have had the effect of producing a political "multiple personality" with adverse consequences for future stable development. The necessity of choice among a multiplicity of options produced in Algeria a tense, unsure, radical society living on the edge of psychological collapse and political upheaval.

A Plebiscitary Democracy

Algeria is presently at a very primitive stage of political development. Possessing little of a genuine historical political character to build on, it has had to fall back upon its colonial experience and a far more primitive Berber regard for communal leadership as inspiration for its current political institutions. What emerged first from this shadowy background was a provisional government (GPRA), which served in exile as a relatively effective coordinating instrument during the revolutionary period but which ignominiously collapsed during the first two chaotic months of independence in the summer of 1962. With the collapse of the provisional government a political bureau composed of five of the original rebel leaders and headed by Ben Bella established itself temporarily as the key governmental institution and assumed the reins of power on September 5, 1962. On the basis of a single list developed by the political bureau, a 190-member national constituent assembly was elected on September 20. A moderate GPRA leader, Ferhat Abbas, was elected president of the assembly, and Ben Bella was invested as premier by a vote of 159 to 1. There were a significant number of abstentions, and a clandestine opposition Socialist Revolutionary party announced its formation.

After his return in November 1962 from a brief American tour Ben Bella began to consolidate his control over the Algerian governmental machinery. Contending that there was no place in Algeria for competing political parties, Ben Bella outlawed the Algerian Communist party. He placed increasing pressure on the national labor union (UGTA), and in January 1963 groups favorable to him won control of the union, which was brought into line with governmental policy.

While Ben Bella was touring the country to explain his nationalization program in the early spring of 1963, the secretary-general of the political bureau, Mohammed Khider, took the opportunity to demand publicly the formation of a mass political party. Upon his return Ben Bella forced Khider to resign. On April 16 he himself assumed the post of secretary-general of the political bureau. In mid-June 1963, following unrest in eastern Algeria, Mohammed Boudiaf, a leading Ben Bella opponent in the political bureau, was arrested along with several army officers for plotting against the security of the state.

Meanwhile under Ben Bella's leadership the National Liberation Front (FLN) prepared a constitution which declared the FLN to be the Algerian nation's supreme guide and only political party. This constitution was submitted to a popular referendum and was approved by 98 per cent of the vote on September 8, 1963.[8] Only in the rebellious Kabylia was the plebiscite effectively boycotted. Just seven days after the approval of the constitution Ben Bella was chosen president for a five-year term by acclamation at a meeting of 3,500 FLN delegates.[9] Thus in the first year of Algerian independence Ben Bella had managed to gain control of all of the main levers of political power in the Algerian nation—the presidency, the secretary-generalship of the party, and the army. The political bureau had ceased to function as an instrument of shared responsibility and had become the tool of a single individual. The national assembly continued to function as an organ of the state, but it had become the rubber stamp of the president. On September 20, 1964, new assembly elections were held on the basis of single slates chosen by the central committee of the FLN. Significantly the 138 delegates chosen for four-year terms were unopposed.

Despite the paper existence of the FLN there was no real oper-

[8] Richard M. Brace, *Morocco-Algeria-Tunisia* (Englewood Cliffs, N.J.: Prentice-Hall, 1964), p. 159.

[9] Ibid.

ating political party with roots in rural Algeria. Party cadres and functionaries existed but not as a formal channel for political action. On the contrary they served merely to duplicate the work of an understaffed bureaucracy. Even between the key elite groups themselves—the president and his brain trust, the army, the national assembly, the FLN, and the students—there was little communication.

Ben Bella had meanwhile been consolidating in the presidential office control of such key administrative posts as the ministries of interior, economic information, and finance, and the government radio and television network.[10] What in fact emerged was a power triumvirate consisting of the peasants (*fellahin*), the Algerian National Army, and the charismatic leader Ben Bella himself.

This continued concentration of power in President Ben Bella's hands was neither surprising nor necessarily detrimental. The predicament facing the developing countries, in the words of a prominent specialist, is that "whatever their constitutional or legal form may be, the political systems of the new and modernizing nations will have strong centralizing and authoritarian tendencies."[11] What was of more concern, however, was whether these strong authoritarian tendencies evidenced by the deposed Algerian regime were becoming totalitarian, or whether they represented a kind of transitory authoritarianism which might augur well for future democratic development.

Unfortunately the political-cultural soil from which Algeria has emerged was comparatively barren of democratic nutriments. Local and indigenous institutions like the tribal structure were either destroyed by the French at an early date or were nonexistent.[12] In addition the French colonial administration bequeathed Algeria a legacy of centralization—a legacy often used as an explanation of the instability of republican and democratic processes in France itself. Moreover the eleventh-hour attempts of France to introduce

[10] *The New York Times*, December 3, 1964, p. 6.

[11] Almond, op. cit.

[12] Charles F. Gallagher, *The United States and North Africa* (Cambridge: Harvard Univ. Press, 1963), p. 65.

democratic plebiscites in Algeria were tarnished by clumsy *Algerie française* tactics and were too late.

President Ben Bella still appeared to hold the crowds by virtue of his charismatic appeal, and he was buttressed by the vital support of the Algerian army. However his isolation from the other political elites of the country became increasingly ominous. Equally disturbing was a growing number of midnight arrests, political imprisonments and executions, and a rising pattern of terrorism. Most troubling of all was the heavy burden of such economic problems as widespread unemployment and declining production both on the farms and in the factories. National unity served Ben Bella as a temporary popular rallying cry, as did the understandable fear of another bloody civil war, but apparently he became overconfident and arrogant.

The Algerian Economy

The current economic picture in Algeria is pessimistic. Outright unemployment exceeds one million—roughly two thirds of the adult work force—and chronic underemployment is rampant. Over-all industrial production has declined 75 per cent since 1961 and is still falling. Commercial activity is stagnating.

There are a few bright aspects of the Algerian economic picture: bumper agricultural crops, continuing savings remittances from metropolitan France by the five hundred thousand Algerian workers living there, and the prospect of rising oil and natural gas revenues as a result of revised profit-sharing arrangements. On balance, however, the situation is bleak, for more than half of the Algerian national budget still comes from foreign aid. France continues to aid the Algerian economy at the rate of $200 million a year; Algeria receives surplus food from the United States at an annual value of about $50 million; the Soviet Union has loaned Algeria $225 million; and Communist China has extended an interest-free credit of $50 million. In all, approximately $1 billion in aid has already reached Algeria.

Perhaps most serious among Algeria's short-run economic problems is the great shortage of technical, entrepreneurial, and professional skills caused by the departure of the Algerian Europeans. A small percentage have remained, and some replacements (mainly teachers) have arrived on a temporary contract basis from metropolitan France. The net outflow of such skills, however, has been little short of catastrophic. Closely related and equally serious has been the declining competence of the Algerian bureaucracy as it has been denuded of its French personnel.

Another major demoralizing factor in the current Algerian economic picture has been the precipitous pace of the nationalization of agriculture, the traditional mainstay of the Algerian economy. At the time of independence the European *colons* produced on two million hectares of land (out of a total of 13 million arable units) 95 per cent of the wine, 90 per cent of the citrus fruit, and more than half the wheat in the entire nation. Not only were the yields of these European-owned farms three to five times higher than those of traditional Moslem farmers, but through their marketing skills the European Algerians were able to dominate access to the European markets.[13]

In the first fifteen months of independence this situation was drastically altered in a three-stage wave of nationalization. In the summer of 1962 approximately one third of *colon* property was abandoned in the rush to leave Algeria. When at last a functioning Algerian government was able to take over in October 1962, the earlier seizures were ratified both to recognize an accomplished fact and to attempt to preserve the unity of the vacated property. The second stage of nationalization occurred in March 1963, when the government issued a decree sequestering many other large European estates. Simultaneously the government, in a manner reminiscent of the romantic French syndicalists, established worker committees to operate the farms and to determine wage rates and the extent of profit-sharing. A state-appointed director was to be responsible for the technical aspects of management. Finally, during the Kabyle revolt at the end of September 1963, the government took over all

[13] Ibid., p. 149.

remaining foreign-owned land. The results of this sweeping nationalization have been little short of disastrous. Despite unusually favorable weather and bumper crops more than 20 per cent of the 1963 wheat harvest was lost and much of the 1963 wine production was not sold, creating major storage problems for the 1964 wine production. The problems are many: lack of funds, lack of skill, lack of equipment, lack of management. Most serious of all has been the tendency of many self-managed farms to ignore the central administration and to go it alone.[14]

Bleak as is this picture of the modernized, formerly European-owned sector of agriculture, the prospects for the million Algerian families eking out a marginal existence on their ancestral plots is even more appalling. To cope with their problems drastic reforms are needed. New pastures must be planted, and grasses must be developed which are suitable for dry areas. Herds of cattle must be rebuilt, breeds improved, and food processing industries launched. Longer term reform programs must be initiated. Institutions similar to American land-grant colleges and the American county agent system might be appropriately adapted to local Algerian conditions. Effective cooperatives and appropriate credit institutions must be developed. Meanwhile much of the Algerian rural population is kept alive at a subsistence level only by virtue of U. S. shipments of surplus wheat.[15] In the long run, however, neither the goal of increasing Algerian agricultural productivity nor dependence on the crutch of foreign food relief are adequate solutions. Population control programs, such as those already underway in Tunisia, are a necessity to check the growth of the Algerian population. Other means must also be found to assist many rural Algerians to find employment in other areas than on the land.

Algeria has also suffered from its haphazard policy of nationalization in industry and commerce without adequate priority planning. Major industries, such as the iron mines and railroads, were nationalized at the very beginning of the independence period. During the Kabyle revolt of September 1963 many small, private enterprises such as hotels, restaurants, and cinemas were also seized.

[14] *The New Republic,* March 14, 1964, p. 11.   [15] Ibid.

At the same time President Ben Bella announced his intention of completely nationalizing all private business. In October 1963 some sixteen hotels which had been peremptorily seized during the Kabyle crisis were returned to their owners, indicating a more conciliatory policy toward some private enterprise.[16] Despite this exception the over-all process of nationalization continues to rush forward. Hundreds of European-owned villas and stores, even tractors and automobiles, have been expropriated by the government. While the domestic political consequences of such actions may have been salutary, the economic consequences have been negative.

Turning to the long-term picture, Algeria has been more fortunate than many underdeveloped countries in the fact that it was provided during the French colonial period with an excellent economic infrastructure—good highways, an integrated railway system, an extensive air network, and a large number of automobiles and trucks per capita. Equally important, it possesses excellent natural resources such as extensive mineral deposits—iron ore, phosphates, petroleum, and natural gas—which have been and are being well developed. Since World War II several light industries such as cement making, paper and textiles industries, tobacco growing, and various types of food processing have developed in Algeria.[17]

In the final days of French rule this incipient industrial capacity was being aggressively promoted under the so-called "Constantine Plan" of 1958, which was designed to bring about the intensive economic development of Algeria by emphasizing housing, education, and industrialization. The plan envisioned the creation within five years of four hundred thousand new industrial jobs, the placing of two thirds of all Algerian children in school, the construction of housing for a million people, the acceleration of oil and natural gas development, and the establishment of chemical and metallurgical industries as a base for further industrialization.[18] The plan failed, in a political sense, mainly because it was too late. The guerrilla war for independence was already too far advanced for the plan to have sufficient impact. The plan also failed to create sufficient new jobs, failed to stimulate sufficient internal investment, and made no

[16] Brace, op. cit., p. 166.   [17] Ibid.   [18] Gallagher, op. cit., p. 163.

real contribution to the problem of dealing with the six million rural Algerians.[19]

Nevertheless the accomplishments of the plan were impressive.[20] At the peak of its operation in 1961 half of Algeria's children were in school, a million new houses had been built, a huge petrochemical industry was under construction, major petroleum and natural gas installations became operative, a cement producing capacity in excess of a million tons a year had been created, and tractor and truck assembly plants had been built. Although the plan officially came to an end with independence, its seeds continue to bear fruit.

In the autumn of 1964 an $80 million plant for processing Algeria's vast resources of natural gas into liquid methane for transportation to Europe was completed near Oran in western Algeria. Construction of a proposed 300,000 ton steel complex at Bone in eastern Algeria has also been resumed. When completed, this project will enable Algeria to produce steel inexpensively by utilizing high-grade iron ore from the Quenza mines and cheap natural gas piped from the Hassi R'mel field.

Taking all the above factors into consideration, the long-term prospects for the Algerian economy appear quite hopeful. Although great problems remain, Algeria does appear to possess a sound foundation for a balanced economy. The interlocking nature of its basic industries seems to constitute a blueprint well adapted to the nation's needs: it should provide the means of improving productivity in agriculture while gradually filtering products out to other, industrial segments of the economy. Using W. W. Rostow's model as a measure, Algeria's economy seems to be roughly halfway between the "feudal stage" and the "take-off stage," with significant elements of both coexisting side by side.

Prospects for Development

Despite its serious economic repercussions the rapid departure of the overwhelming majority of Algerian Europeans did have the side-effect of almost eliminating what would probably have consti-

[19] Ibid., pp. 163–64.   [20] Ibid.

tuted a very large, obstreperous, and powerful minority in the Algerian nation—a minority which might have placed substantial obstacles in the path of achieving national unity. To this extent the European exodus was a blessing in disguise, particularly since the last-ditch terrorist campaign of the settler-sponsored secret army (O.A.S.) left behind many scars.

Another major source of opposition to the achievement of Algerian national unity developed as a result of the fragmentation of the revolutionary leadership itself. Moderates such as Ferhat Abbas resigned from the government and predicted that the one-party regime instituted by Ben Bella "will be condemned by the very nature of things to evolve toward Fascist structures."[21] On the other hand Leftist critics such as Mohammed Boudiaf criticized the regime as not truly doctrinaire but "pseudo-Socialistic."[22] The most serious and continued opposition to national unity came from the one-million Berber minority in the mountains of the Grand Kabylia. It was in this area that the first revolt against the regime broke out, and it is here that opposition has been simmering ever since. The motives of this opposition are mixed—an amalgam of provincial and ethnic pride, extreme poverty, and the personal ambitions of local leaders such as Hoçine Ait Ahmed and Colonel El Hadj.

For a time, it appeared that the charismatic leadership of Ben Bella had been able to impose a genuine sense of national unity upon the young nation. This was no mean achievement for a state literally born of revolutionary chaos and with only a dim historical past to recall. The coup on June 19, 1965, however, casts considerable doubt upon the reality and strength of this apparent sense of national unity.

The question of ideology is something else again. Ben Bella stated: "We want an Algerian socialism which is based on our own experience and, at the same time, also draws on that of the Socialist countries. . . ."[23] On its face this approach implied the adoption of a "pragmatic Socialism" which would be responsive to local condi-

---

[21] *The New York Times,* September 29, 1963, p. 31.   [22] Ibid.

[23] Paul E. Sigmund, Jr., *The Ideologies of the Developing Nations* (New York: Praeger, 1963), p. 146.

tions—a program which, while recognizing the need for drastic reforms in Algerian society, might have pursued this objective in a practical rather than a doctrinaire fashion.

In the immediate postindependence period there were hopeful signs that such was to be the approach. While the de facto situation of the abandoned agricultural lands required state intervention to preserve the indivisibility of the settler holdings, Ben Bella had reassured Europeans in November 1962 that they had nothing to fear for their business enterprises. Within six months, however, large-scale nationalization was underway that affected Algerian Moslems as well as Europeans. In direct reaction to the Kabyle revolt in September 1963 the nationalization process was made even more comprehensive. The Ben Bella regime had thus moved very rapidly to the left, seemingly substituting a doctrinaire Socialist approach for a pragmatic one.

What are the practical consequences of this policy? The result has been to scare off desperately needed foreign credit and investment not only by the danger of nationalization but also by creating an atmosphere of uncertainty. Ben Bella's increasingly doctrinaire ideology was a major brake on Algerian economic development.

Initially Algeria seemed fortunate to possess a charismatic leader like Ben Bella. By no means an intellectual, Ben Bella appeared to display consummate political skill not only in attaining power but also in dealing with the recurrent crises which beset him. However, political leadership in the modern state must ultimately be something more than a one-man show. It was in this respect that the deposed Algerian government left much to be desired. The original leadership elite which sponsored the revolution had been decimated by death, exile, and arrests. The nationalist party (FLN) had become a subservient rubber stamp which served to ratify rather than to develop policy. The Algerian civil service was on the whole inexperienced and ineffective. Only the army, through the influence of then Vice-President and Defense Minister Houari Boumedienne, appeared to exercise any significant influence on the determination of national policy.

The major contemporary issue in Algerian politics prior to the coup was the struggle between the "Arabists" and the "Marxists" within the FLN itself. The first group advocated continuing and strengthening the Islamic tradition in Algerian society. The second, while not Communist per se, leaned strongly toward the introduction and application of Marxist concepts to Algerian development. Ben Bella attempted to straddle these groups and keep above them, retaining the support of both. When a choice had to be made, however, he consistently supported the "Arabists" rather than the "Marxists." The first significant evidence of this policy came in November 1962, when he outlawed the Algerian Communist party. Another came when he dismissed a leading Marxist from the editorship of *Révolution Africaine* in August 1964. In the fall of 1964 Islamic instruction was made compulsory in all Algerian public schools. The most recent example of this Ben Bella technique occurred on January 21, 1965, when he published an article in the Algerian labor weekly *Révolution et Travail*. In the article he denounced both Communism and anti-Communism and wrote that Algeria had adopted "a Marxian economic analysis but has not adopted Marxist ideology because Algerians are Moslems and Arabs."[24] The new regime appears to be strongly "Arabist" in orientation.

The Boumedienne Coup

Causes

Early in the morning of June 19, 1965, President Ben Bella was arrested on the orders of Vice-President and Defense Minister Houari Boumedienne. Coming as it did on the eve of the so-called "Second Bandung Conference" of Afro-Asian countries, with Ben Bella seemingly at the height of his prestige, the coup took the world by surprise. Although it had long been assumed that the Army constituted the main buttress of Ben Bella's support, most observers had characterized the shy, reserved Boumedienne as an *éminence grise* content to wield power and exercise influence behind the throne.

[24] *The New York Times,* January 22, 1965, p. 4.

What then caused the sudden coup? Apparently Ben Bella, made somewhat overconfident by the consciousness of his growing international prestige, became incautious and arrogant. He not only demanded the removal of Foreign Minister Abdelaziz Bouteflika, a friend and ally of Colonel Boumedienne, but it was also rumored that Ben Bella intended subsequently to remove the defense minister himself. Hearing of the plot, Boumedienne acted immediately before the conference, lest Ben Bella's prestige become too great and his removal more embarrassing, if not impossible.

While the self-preservation motive triggered the coup, there were undoubtedly several other justifications for it. Perhaps most significant was the fact that Algeria's economy has continued to be stagnant with an oppressively high degree of unemployment. The stark reality of economic stagnation was probably aggravated by Ben Bella's costly grandstand role in international and Afro-Asian affairs. For example, the cost of preparations for both the Afro-Asian conference and the Ninth World Youth Festival obviously constituted a major diversion of scarce economic resources desperately needed in other sectors of the sagging Algerian economy. Second, increasing concern about the role and influence exercised by the Marxists and the Communists in the Ben Bella regime was also undoubtedly disturbing to the Algerian "Arabists," even though previously Ben Bella had always sided with them at critical moments. Moreover in the last few weeks of his rule Ben Bella appeared to be attempting to pacify and to gain the support of some of his former political enemies. Former Premier Ferhat Abbas was released after a year's detention in the Sahara, as were several other "old-guard" political prisoners. There was also speculation that Ben Bella was attempting to achieve reconciliation with his long-time guerrilla adversary Hoçine Ait Ahmed. Similarly "there were reports that the deposed president planned to bring Belkaçem Krim, a Kabyle leader and a long-standing foe of Colonel Boumedienne, back into the government."[25] One could have interpreted these moves as an attempt to build political counterweights against the power of the army. There was undoubtedly the fear that Ben Bella might attempt to reduce the size of the 60,000-man Algerian army. In the past Ben Bella had

[25] *The New York Times,* June 20, 1965, p. 2.

talked casually of the desirability of creating a people's militia, which would be adequate for the nation's postindependence security needs. Clearly expenditures for the maintenance of such a large army do constitute a major charge and a heavy burden on the Algerian economy, and therefore they present an attractive opportunity for budget reductions.

Finally, the coup was undoubtedly fostered by a growing hatred of Ben Bella himself felt increasingly "by other members of the leadership. They accused the President of being authoritarian and power-hungry," and of attempting to develop a cult of personality.[26]

Significance

Despite early student protest demonstrations against it, the new Algerian regime seems to possess significant elements of stability. The army is the most powerful and cohesive force in Algeria. Most of the ruling leadership elite appear to have accepted the change without significant objection and to have been "carried over." Only the Communists and Marxists appear to be actively intriguing for Ben Bella's return.

According to informed diplomatic sources, "the Revolutionary Council appeared to be heading toward collective leadership,"[27] the approach utilized by the FLN during the rebellion. In a recent interview Ahmed Kaid, the new Algerian chief of information services, "stressed the collegial nature of the regime and declared that Colonel Boumedienne was not the 'President or the Chairman.' "[28] Another source close to the revolutionary council commented that "it is the style and the management that have changed, not the basic policies."[29]

Algerian foreign policy under the new regime may become more realistic. "Algeria is expected to continue to side with radical African, Arab, and Asian states, but without simply echoing the Moscow or Cairo line and without making spectacular new bids for 'revolutionary' prestige abroad." Good relations with France are to receive

[26] Ibid. [27] *The New York Times,* June 30, 1965, p. 7.
[28] Ibid. [29] Ibid.

priority attention, and the regime has already warned against external interference in Algerian internal affairs. Domestically the new regime is expected to concentrate on the economic crisis. It is believed that it will "seek to consolidate and revamp its chaotic 'worker self-management' system at home with less dependence on Marx and more stress on Islam."[30]

While spokesmen for the regime are stressing continuity of policy, an attitude which has been characterized as "Ben Bellaism without Ben Bella," a more dominant theme seems to be simply genuine independence. "We want to be ourselves," said a high-placed official close to the revolutionary council.

What practical consequences for Algerian development may such changes have? Hopefully Algeria may be able to put its domestic house more in order by reducing unemployment, by encouraging more private capital investment, by cutting wasteful "prestige" expenditures, and possibly by securing additional free-world economic assistance. Despite past controversies a less prestige-conscious Algeria might even be able to develop useful cooperative devices with its neighbors, Tunisia and Morocco, such as a North African customs union.

On the other hand the dominance of military power in a political context always raises the possibility of a continuing military dictatorship. As the strongest power center in Algerian society the army could abuse its power and perpetuate its control either consciously or subconsciously in its own interests. Conversely the army could become—as it has in many other less developed areas of the world—a major modernizing force, utilizing its discipline, organization, and technology for progressive, developmental purposes. The ascetic demeanor of Colonel Boumedienne suggests that he is no Bonaparte, but rather a dedicated, self-effacing, nationalistic reformer. This is a hopeful aspect. More troubling, however, is the significance of Colonel Boumedienne's traditional Moslem background and education. Organized religion is always a conservative force in the life of any nation. Certainly intensified respect for Islamic tradition would be evidenced in any regime supported actively by him. To

[30] Ibid.

what extent this fact would inhibit cultural change and the modernization of Algerian society is difficult to assess *in futuro,* but it must be considered.

One final caveat: the many changes wrought in Algerian society over the last three years are unlikely to be undone quickly, if indeed at all. Modifications of and, hopefully, improvements in policy are all that one may realistically anticipate from the new regime. From its initial announcement of the coup the regime made clear that it would carry on the "revolution." Communist intrigue and heavy-handedness might, however, push it almost unwillingly in a Western direction—mainly toward its natural sponsor, France.

SELECTED BIBLIOGRAPHY

BARBOUR, N. *A Survey of Northwest Africa (the Maghrib).* London: Oxford Univ. Press, 1962.

BEHR, E. *The Algerian Problem.* New York: Norton, 1961.

BOURDIEU, PIERRE. *The Algerians.* Boston: Beacon, 1962.

BRACE, RICHARD M. *Morocco-Algeria-Tunisia.* Englewood Cliffs, N.J.: Prentice-Hall, 1964.

CLARK, MICHAEL K. *Algeria in Turmoil.* New York: Praeger, 1959.

GALLAGHER, CHARLES F. *The United States and North Africa.* Cambridge: Harvard Univ. Press, 1963.

GILLESPIE, JOAN. *Algeria: Rebellion and Revolutions.* New York: Praeger, 1961.

GORDON, DAVID. *North Africa's French Legacy, 1954–1962.* Cambridge: Harvard Univ. Press, 1962.

KRAFT, JOSEPH. *Struggle for Algeria.* New York: Doubleday, 1961.

PAWERA, JOHN C. *Algeria's Infrastructure.* New York: Praeger, 1964.

TILLION, GERMAINE. *Algeria: The Realities.* New York: Knopf, 1958.

———. *France and Algeria, Complementary Enemies.* New York: Knopf, 1961.

ZARTMAN, I. WILLIAM. *Government and Politics in North Africa.* New York: Praeger, 1963.

Tunisia

Tunisia is a relatively small country of only 48,300 square miles, occupying a strategic position on the North African coast. Situated in the center of the Mediterranean basin, flanked on the west by Algeria and on the southwest by Libya, Tunisia lies approximately halfway between the Straits of Gibraltar and the Suez Canal. Its coastline extends along the Mediterranean for eight hundred miles, and at its closest point to Europe it is only 85 miles from Sicily. The Atlas Mountains divide the country into a well-watered north and an arid south that extends into the Sahara. Its population in 1963 was 4,168,000, of whom 140,000 were European (predominantly French and Italian). The remaining 90 per cent are of Arab and Berber descent and are of the Moslem faith.

Under the pretext of protecting French national security in Algeria, France in 1881 resorted to military intervention in Tunisia and forced the reigning bey to accept the Treaty of Bardo. This treaty, and the subsequent Treaty of LaMarsa in 1883, established what was in theory a protectorate government. In actuality Tunisia was reduced to colonial status, with the bey in nominal control but with actual authority vested in the French resident-general. During the colonial period (1881–1956) the French made substantial contributions to Tunisia's economy. The French installed the machinery of a modern administrative state and inaugurated numerous public improvements, including an educational system and hospitals as well as the beginnings of an adequate railroad and highway system. The incipient mining industry was promoted by extensive prospecting of phosphate and iron ore deposits located in the south. Yet despite the substantial contributions made by the French, their policy in regard to Tunisia was primarily one of economic exploitation geared to augment the wealth of the French landowners. Little was done to aid the Tunisian peasants.

Political Development

Modern political development in Tunisia dates from 1907, when a European-educated intelligensia, capitalizing on the discontent arising from economic grievances and the resentment of European discrimination, formed the Young Tunisians party. In 1920 a new party, the Destour (Tunisian Party of the Constitution), was formed which proclaimed Tunisia's right to emancipation as a nation. The Destour party lacked discipline and effective organization and was eventually eclipsed in 1934 by the more modern and dynamic Neo-Destour party led by Habib Bourguiba. Bourguiba aimed at complete independence. However his strategy, now appropriately labeled "Bourguibism," advocated decolonialization in stages through peaceful negotiations and compromise. Neo-Destour's first objective—internal autonomy—was not realized until July 31, 1954, when the French by the Declaration of Carthage abandoned their policy of cosovereignty. Additional negotiations followed, but it was not until March 20, 1956, that Tunisia attained complete independence. Almost immediately steps were taken to build a new political order. A constituent assembly of ninety members was elected for a term of five years, a constitution was framed, and French administrators were gradually replaced by Tunisians. On July 25, 1957, the reigning bey, Sidi Lamine, was deposed, and Tunisia was declared a republic by the constituent assembly. Habib Bourguiba was unanimously elected president of the new constitutional Islamic republic.

Tunisia's greatest asset is her political stability. How was this achieved? Great credit is due the able and charismatic leadership of Bourguiba himself, who molded his party and the young generation to his image of an independent Tunisia. Charles Micaud analyzes this phenomenon in greater detail:

Tunisia has reached a high degree of political integration. There is no wide gap separating the small urban elite and the large traditionalist masses, as there is in most transitional societies. The party has had a broad popular base, and has succeeded in creating a near consensus on the goals and methods of modernization. The importance of non-economic factors in the process of modernization has been clearly demonstrated from the emergence of the small aristocratic elite of Young Tunisians at the turn of the century to the formation of a broad political elite of Neo-Destourian cadres. . . . With this wide base, the party could successfully mobilize the masses in the cities and the countryside, first in the struggle for independence and later in the battle against underdevelopment.[1]

Micaud emphasizes the key role of education in this context of political mobilization. The Neo-Destour party was and continues to be a major instrument of political education and social integration. Formal education, institutional reform (the emancipation of women), and planning—all these were components of the excellent program of social engineering undertaken in Tunisia.

Still another important aspect of Tunisia's political development is the role played by the one-party system. Micaud asserts that this system by "allowing a minimum of democracy at the beginning, in fact prepares the way for a more mature phase of democratic role through the competition of organized political forces. Here the concept of consensus is essential to an understanding of the role that can be played by a single party in a transitional society. Agreement on basic values must be reached before a competition of parties can be safe and creative. Otherwise, the dialogue between traditionalists and modernists can only lead to an embittered and largely meaningless struggle opening the way to demagogy and preventing the modern nation state from being built on a foundation of active consent."[2]

Tunisia has, however, had its opposition groups. The chief opposition to Bourguiba came from the one-time general secretary of the Neo-Destour party, Salah Ben Youssef, who denounced Bourguiba's gradualism as a sellout to colonialism. Although expelled from the party, Youssef was permitted to expound his views for a few months in 1955. When the Neo-Destour Congress in mid-

[1] Charles A. Micaud, *Tunisia: The Politics of Modernization* (New York: Praeger, 1964), pp. 187–88.
[2] Ibid., p. 188.

November 1955 endorsed Bourguiba's policies, however, Youssef "declared war" on the government and resorted to terrorism and armed uprising. It required some six months to pacify the remnants of his guerrilla army in the south. He was assassinated in Frankfurt on August 12, 1961. Clement Moore has pointed out: "The history of Youssefism has had serious consequences for Tunisia. The general atmosphere of insecurity that it created reinforced authoritarism trends within the party and government. The chaos resulting from open disagreements on fundamental issues forced most Tunisians to conclude that national unity transcended all other goals."[3] Other public critics of the government, such as Ben Salah, leader of the Tunisian trade union movement, and Mohammed Masmoudi, have been disciplined for their powerful criticism and then returned to grace in new jobs.

At best Tunisia could be described as a tutelary democracy. Both the Neo-Destour party and the national assembly remain politically subordinate to President Bourguiba. They are important only in so far as they have potentialities as democratic institutions. At the local level the party has developed a very healthy democratic political process. More than a thousand local branches of the party have been established, representing the people and giving them an opportunity to manage many of their local affairs. Town councils were instituted in 1957, and in small villages the town council and the party branch may be identical in membership. But it is important to note that political participation has been meaningfully extended to the masses and that democratic forms are generally respected at the local level, where the people are encouraged to discuss problems with which they are most familiar. Moreover it is now apparent that the single-party regime, which fostered local democracy, is now attempting to extend the new political approach into a more broad-based national political process. While Bourguiba's presence is very much needed now, it is probable that a new style of national politics more dependent upon institutions will emerge once he retires. On the whole, then, the prospects for political development in Tunisia seem quite hopeful in comparison with the situation existing in many less developed states.

[3] Ibid., p. 91.

Economic Development

The Tunisian economy is basically the agricultural type common in the Mediterranean area, with wheat, wine, olive oil, and citrus fruit constituting the principal produce. Moreover this economy, similar to that of both Algeria and Morocco, is essentially a dual one: there is a modern, European, commercial sector and an older, primitive, indigenous sector—and the two sectors coexist side by side with little mobility between them. The Europeans dominate the specialty fields in Tunisia; they grow half of all the wheat, 75 per cent of the citrus fruit, and 90 per cent of the wine.[4] The last refuge of the traditional agriculturists has been stock raising, which accounts for approximately 20 per cent of the nation's gross agricultural income. The indigenous agriculturist is condemned to a precarious livelihood by archaic farming methods, inadequate land distribution, and unfavorable climatic conditions. Lack of water, for example, is a very serious problem, especially in the arid southern regions of the country.

On the industrial side, Tunisia must rely chiefly on her phosphate production, which amounts to more than two million tons annually. Phosphates account for 30 per cent of Tunisia's total exports and make her the world's fourth largest producer. Tunisia also has substantial iron ore reserves, and in 1961 it produced 848 million tons. But Tunisia lacks coal, and an extensive search has not revealed any appreciable quantity of oil. Because of the lack of large rivers hydroelectric power is also not feasible. Therefore a modest industrial development begun since World War II has been retarded by the lack of any source of cheap power, and this deficiency in industrial development accounts in part for the country's huge annual trade deficit. In 1961 imports amounted to $210 million, and exports amounted to $110 million; this left a balance of payments deficit of approximately $100 million.[5]

The French economic legacy to Tunisia had been the typical colonial one: a costly and modern façade, lopsided development,

[4] Charles F. Gallagher, *The United States and North Africa* (Cambridge: Harvard Univ. Press, 1963), p. 149.
[5] Ibid.

and an undeveloped infrastructure. In addition Tunisia relied heavily on French trade. France provided a cheap market for her goods and helped cover Tunisia's annual trade deficit. When Bourguiba's sympathy with the Algerian revolt precipitated the withdrawal of French financial aid in May 1957, the newly formed government was faced with a herculean task of serious economic reorientation. Charles F. Gallagher analyzed the situation this way:

The basic problem is the lack of employment which goes back to the crisis on the land: too many people are doing too little on land insufficient in quantity and often indaequate in quality. Because of the rapidly increasing population the situation in the countryside goes from bad to worse, and there are only three general ways to escape. One is to make the relationship between the population and the land more bearable by the adjustment and redistribution of existing acreage (land reform). A second is to make better utilization of existing areas (increased cultivation) through improved techniques (increased productivity). Another is to increase the available amount of land by the reclamation of unused or marginal regions or added irrigation. These solutions employ agrarian measures exclusively, but they may be combined with a fourth . . . providing employment in a new urban environment. This means the development of an industrial economy and a planned campaign of investment to achieve it.[6]

Gallagher might well have added population control to the first alternative. For perhaps the most crucial problem facing Tunisia today is its prolific birth rate. Improved health conditions have resulted in a steady lowering of the death rate, which has in turn produced a population increase of 2 per cent annually. In 1963 Tunisia was regarded as having one of the youngest populations in the world, 50 per cent being under 19 years of age.

Tunisia has in fact placed most stress upon the first and second alternatives for reform with some experimentation in the third. A far-reaching land reform was begun in 1956, and under it the state has acquired the tribal land-holdings, which amount to one quarter of the cultivated area in the country. Simultaneously some four million acres of tribal lands were shifted to individual holders.

[6] Ibid., pp. 155–56.

And since 1960, except during the Bizerte crisis, the state has been purchasing the property held by European settlers.[7]

In the interest of population control the Tunisian government has undertaken several interrelated measures. Polygamy has been prohibited, and women have been granted equal status with men. Following intensive study the government opened a birth control campaign with a press and radio barrage. Simultaneously it raised the legal minimum age for marriage from 18 to 20 for men and from 15 to 17 for women.

Appreciating that modernization presupposes great transformations in individual and social attitudes, President Bourguiba has improved and extended the educational system inaugurated by the French. Education has moved from religious to state control, and not only is the next generation being educated, but a crash program of training agricultural technicians is underway on a large scale. In fourteen secondary schools devoted to agricultural instruction there were 2,500 students in 1964. By 1970 Tunisia expects to have educated 540 agricultural engineers, 400 agricultural administrators, 1,200 technical assistants, 3,700 agricultural monitors, and 5,800 lower grade agricultural specialists.

To meet the problem of chronic high unemployment—one out of every three workers—Bourguiba launched in 1959 a large-scale program of public works called the "Battle Against Underdevelopment."[8] Designed to substitute labor for capital by utilizing the unemployed on public works projects, the program had an important secondary aim of preventing migration to urban slums. More than 150,000 workers have been utilized for projects such as urban renewal, building roads, digging wells, constructing small earthworks and dams to retain rain waters, building irrigation canals and erosion and flood control works, and implementing a reforestation plan.

On August 23, 1961, President Bourguiba announced the Ten-Year Perspective for Development.[9] This perspective sets forth four fundamental objectives. The first is the "Tunisification" of the economy, that is, reduction of Tunisia's dependence on France for

[7] Ibid., p. 159.   [8] Micaud, p. 174.   [9] Ibid., p. 176.

trade and a decrease in the foreign component of the financial, industrial, and agricultural sectors of the economy. The second objective is raising the standard of living for the masses, the third is a reform of the basic structures of the economy, and the final goal is attainment of self-sustained growth. Quantitatively the perspective proposes the achievement of an annual growth rate of 6 per cent, a gross national product of $1.157 million, a rationed income per capita of $107—all by 1971. In addition the plan proposes to increase investment in the south and central parts of the country. These areas comprise four-fifths of the land and contain 30 per cent of the population, but historically they have been neglected because of the paucity of known resources in these areas.

The first phase—the Three-Year Plan, launched early in 1962— has the following optimistic targets: agricultural production to be raised 40 per cent above the average output for recent years, industrial production to be double that of 1957, total employment to be reached in 1964, and domestic savings to rise from 10 to 20 per cent of the gross national product.

In considering both the perspective and the three-year plan it is quite apparent that they are overly optimistic and ambitious, particularly in respect to the rate of growth, investment, and domestic savings. Yet to the extent that they are pragmatic and not doctrinaire, flexible and not final, that they have attempted to reconcile the great conflicting objectives of maximum growth, social justice, and individual freedom, they deserve high praise.[10]

Developmental Prospects

Tunisia's over-all developmental prospects are good. In addition to its original asset of a relatively cohesive and settled society, Tunisia has had the good fortune of enjoying political stability and excellent leadership. President Bourguiba has competence and vision as well as charisma. The Neo-Destour party is extremely mature and competent. It has not only developed a realistic program to meet national needs, but it has also carefully explained and justified this program to all segments of the population. The result

[10] Ibid., p. 185.

is that despite grave political storms like the Bizerte crisis in 1961, Bourguiba and the Neo-Destour party have been able to retain the confidence of the nation.

The economic picture in Tunisia is much less auspicious for both the long and the short run. Tunisia lacks exploitable sources of energy—coal, oil, and water power. Much of its soil is barren or almost so. It has a large amount of traditional subsistence economy, a minimal degree of industrialization, and a low income per capita. Despite its creative efforts at modernization and the resultant U.S. financial help with its ambitious Ten-Year Plan, it faces grave problems: (1) the scarcity of skilled technical, managerial, and professional personnel; (2) government controls which tend to discourage would-be entrepreneurs from risk-taking in the industrial sector; (3) the small size of the domestic market, which seems to preclude low-cost production of many manufactured goods; (4) the selection of investment priorities not only in terms of sector and area but also in terms of the type of investment; (5) the choice of "Tunisification" and foreign investment or national sovereignty and transnational ties; and (6) the ability to slow down its present high birth rate. Given, however, its social and political cohesion, its balanced and wise planning, and the financial support of the United States, it would seem that Tunisia stands a good chance of surviving the period of "foreign dole" and of eventually attaining the so-called "take-off stage" of economic growth.

SELECTED BIBLIOGRAPHY

BARBOUR, N. A Survey of Northwest Africa (the Maghrib). London: Oxford Univ. Press, 1962.

BRACE, RICHARD M. Morocco-Algeria-Tunisia. Englewood Cliffs, N.J.: Prentice-Hall, 1964.

GALLAGHER, C. F. The United States and North Africa. Cambridge, Mass.: Harvard Univ. Press, 1963.

GORDON, DAVID. North Africa's French Legacy, 1954–1962. Cambridge, Mass.: Harvard Univ. Press, 1962.

MICAUD, C. A. Tunisia: The Politics of Modernization. New York: Praeger, 1964.

MOORE, C. H. The Dynamics of One-Party Government: Tunisia Since Independence. Berkeley: Univ. of California Press, 1965.

India

India, the largest nation in South Asia, has an estimated population of 462 million people (550 million by 1971) and an area of 1,262,275 square miles. It has a tropical, monsoon climate with considerable variations from the Himalayan highlands to the coastal areas. More than 85 per cent of the population adheres to the Hindu religion; 10 per cent are Moslem, 2 per cent Christian, 2 per cent Sikh, and 1 per cent other. The estimated annual rate of growth of the Indian population is 2.2 per cent. Approximately 75 per cent of India's people are still illiterate, and the average income per capita is $70 annually. More than 80 per cent of the Indian population earn their living through agriculture and live on village plots of less than five acres. Although the "state of untouchability" has been legally outlawed, the caste system still prevails in most areas of the country.

Under the Official Languages Act of 1963 English was to be the official Indian language only until January 26, 1963, at which time Hindi was to take its place. This fact provoked bloody riots in South India during the early part of 1965 and caused the Shastri government to back away from an absolutist position on the language issue. It is therefore important to note that fourteen languages are recognized by the Indian constitution of 1950—Assamese, Bengali, Gujarati, Hindi, Kannada, Kashmiri, Malayalam, Marathi, Oriya, Panjabi, Sanskrit, Tamil, Telugu, and Urdu.

After more than two hundred years of British colonial rule India received its independence on August 15, 1947, but not without bloodshed. Two independent states were established—India and Pakistan. A complete division of the population, area, civil service, and armed forces had to take place. Over eleven million refugees migrated in both directions. Transportation and communications were disrupted, migrants found themselves jobless and destitute, and the resulting economic situation was almost catastrophic for both new nations. Some five hundred princely states then had to be united into viable units. Kashmir, a province headed by a Hindu prince but including a Moslem majority in its population that was forced to accede to India, became an international problem at this time as a result of the violent separation. This problem is still unsettled.

National Unity and Ideology

Except for the unsolved Kashmir problem the violent separation of the two great religious groups and the exchange of refugees did have the ultimate side effect of producing a strong sense of national unity in India today. This is particularly important in view of India's size and huge population as well as the fact that over 200 languages and dialects are spoken and very significant religious minorities are still present within the country. The Indian constitution of 1950 describes India as a "democratic secular state," which implies a state which respects individual and corporate freedom of religion and which deals with the individual as a citizen irrespective of his religion. This provision, in practice, is nothing more than a pious platitude. Hinduism both permeates and dominates Indian society.

India's economic ideology is basically a democratic socialism, resembling that of the British Labor party. In the more than 500,000 villages which constitute the bulk of India's economy, land is privately owned and worked, however. The Indian industrial economy is mixed with significant elements of both private enterprise and state control. The new prime minister, Shastri, is regarded very much as a middle-of-the-road pragmatic politician who will attempt to follow Nehru's course rather than any strong ideological direction of his own.

Political Development

Indian nationalism began in 1885 with the founding of the Indian National Congress. The Moslem counterpart of the Congress, the Moslem League, was founded in 1906. These movements led to the Morley Minto Reforms of 1909, which gave elected seats to Indians for service on provincial councils. At the same time the "seeds of partition" were sown by separating the elections of Hindus and Moslems. The Act of 1919 set up a quasi-federal system with a bicameral legislature, composed of the Council of State and the Assembly, at the national level. Further pressure by the nationalists for concessions from the British led to violence. After World War I, however, Mohandas K. Gandhi began preaching his doctrine of non-violent noncooperation, thus giving a moral and spiritual aura to the movement for nationalism and attempting to unite Hindus and Moslems. After a period in jail he was politically inactive for a time, during which Jawaharlal Nehru appeared as a militant nationalist leader. In 1928 Gandhi returned to politics, and a year later he received a pledge from the Indian national government to set a tentative date (January 26, 1949) for Indian independence. This led to conferences in London in 1930 to discuss the problems and issues in India, which at that time was engaged in nationwide civil disobedience campaigns. These conferences led to the British act of 1935 that granted added powers to provincial and central governments in India.

In November 1939 all the Congress ministers resigned objecting to the circumstances whereby Britain had brought India into World War II. In 1940 the Moslems, moving further and further from unity with the Congress, adopted the Lahore Resolution to form separate states in areas of Moslem majority. The Moslem League also gave all-out support to the British in her war effort, while Congress launched nonviolent protests to oppose Britain. Throughout the war the two groups continued thus divided, and partition of India became inevitable. When the war ended and the Labor party came to power in 1945, plans continued for granting India independence by 1948. Nehru was asked to form an interim government in a last attempt to join the Congress and the Moslem League in a united India, but these efforts failed.

Today India has both a parliamentary system patterned after Britain and a federal structure. It has a president, vice-president, prime minister, and a bicameral Parliament. The upper house, the Council of States, has twelve members who are nominated by the president and 250 other members chosen by the sixteen state assemblies. The lower house, the House of the People, has five hundred members directly elected under universal adult suffrage. There is a Council of Ministers, which is dominated by the prime minister and the Congress party who together make all major decisions in the government today.

There are five major political parties or groupings in India today. First, there is the Indian National Congress party, led by Gandhi and Nehru in the past, which has dominated the political scene since independence. Nehru concentrated on national unity and left much of the responsibility for internal affairs to his deputy prime minister. Nehru also moved gradually toward a mild socialism, calling for state ownership and control of production and "equal distribution of national wealth." Some observers feel that effective democracy is unlikely with the continued dominance of the Congress party, and many are dubious of the party's viability now that Nehru is dead.

The Swatantra (Freedom) party is a conservative, noncommunal, anti-Communist party. It was formed in 1959 in opposition to socialism. As yet it represents no real opposition to Congress, and it will not unless and until it should gain members from among dissatisfied, conservative Congress party members.

The Communal parties such as the Jan Sangh are made up of various Hindu factions and are devoted to the interests of the untouchables and other more limited causes. Taken as a whole they have been relatively unsuccessful at the national level and have enjoyed only random local successes. Recent electoral victories of the Jan Sangh party, however, have made it a political force of real significance.

The Indian Socialist party, founded in 1934, remained "under the roof" of the Congress party until 1948, when it became an independent political group. Following the 1952 general election, it joined with the Kisan Mazdoor Praja party (KMPP) in the hope of becoming the principal opposition party in the Indian Parliament.

However, these hopes have not been fulfilled. Plagued by dissension and preoccupied by ideology, the so-called Praja Socialist party split in 1955, losing at least 30 per cent of its supporters to the Independent Socialist party. The leadership of the PSP has been decimated by death, disillusionment, and defection. Its morale is low; its short-term prospects, dubious. In large measure, the difficulties of genuine Indian socialism stem from the fact that Nehru himself had strong socialist sympathies, and was able to preempt much of the potential appeal of the Socialist party for his own Congress party.

The Communist party, the largest opposition to the Congress party in Parliament, has never yet held more than thirty seats in the House of the People. Its underground component, however, is extensive. Communism, of course, appeals to many who are dissatisfied with slow economic development and improvement and who are impressed by the economic progress of the Soviet Union and Red China. The "educated unemployed" are also widely attracted to Communism. In 1964, the Indian Communist party split into two separate parties because of tensions resulting from the Sino-Soviet rift; one of the new parties is pro-Soviet, the other pro-Communist Chinese. In December 1964 the Indian government arrested more than one thousand members of the pro-Communist Chinese party for plotting against the government. In the last election the united Communist party polled 10 per cent of the popular vote, drawing its main support from trade unions, student groups, and peasant groups. It constituted the only effective opposition to the Congress party at the national level. At the local level there are many regional groupings and tribal organizations, but thus far they have not succeeded in becoming effective political forces.

Elections so far have shown a turnout of more than 50 per cent of the electorate. Because so many of the people are illiterate, special symbols on multiple ballot boxes were used, and the voter dropped a coded ballot into the box of his party choice. In 1962 paper ballots with candidates' names and party symbols were marked in secret by the voter. This was slower and more confusing for illiterates, but it was also relatively successful. The people are slowly beginning to participate in politics and to be articulate on issues of national importance such as the Goa dispute and the establishment of linguistic states. However they still cling to the ancient belief in *darshan,* or the beneficial effect of being in the presence of a great man. This directly affects politics (perhaps to the detriment of democratic development); for example, it accounted for the almost childlike faith of the Indian people in the wisdom of Nehru.

On balance, however, the prospects for Indian political development seem reasonably optimistic. Despite such significant deterrent factors as poverty and illiteracy, progress toward mass participation in the political process seems very hopeful. The charismatic leadership of Nehru and the quiet succession of the colorless but apparently competent Shastri have provided India with the essential ingredient of effective leadership. Even the relatively limited Indian political party system stands well in comparison with the political systems existing in most of the other newly independent nations.

Economic Development

Agriculture

India is a predominately agricultural country which still cannot feed itself because of chronic crop failures resulting from the unpredictability of the monsoons. The fertility of the land is dependent upon the timeliness of the monsoon rains except in those few areas where irrigation is employed. India also suffers from a troublesome landlord problem: a small minority of 10 per cent owns more than half of all cultivated land. The remaining landowners average less than 7.5 acres with low yields per acre. Eighty per cent of all arable land is in use, and only 20 per cent of this is irrigated. Millet, rice, and wheat are grown on 65 per cent of the land under cultivation, but these cereal crops are not sufficient to maintain a well-nourished population. Cattle are raised solely as sacred animals because of the predominant Hindu religion, and therefore they do not constitute a food product. Over-all, India raises approximately

159 million cattle, 45 million buffaloes, 39 million sheep, and 4.9 million pigs.

Since India has an annual growth rate of 2.2 per cent, or approximately nine million people per year, Indian agriculture is not able to break away from its subsistence level. Total production has risen about 2.5 per cent since 1950, but this scarcely balances the increase in population. Accordingly, some observers have advocated that the Indian government shift the emphasis of public investment allocation toward the agricultural sector, thereby helping the autonomous elements there to attain the preconditions for growth sufficient to sustain a rapidly expanding population.

The demand for land reform in India has met much resistance. Cooperative farming is opposed on the grounds that it is against tradition and individual rights. The voluntary movement for "land gift," or *bhoodan,* was initiated in 1951 by Acharya Vinoba Bjave, a follower of Gandhi. This man, known as the "walking saint," has walked thousands of miles seeking voluntary donations of one sixth of a landowner's plot for redistribution to the landless. He has broadened the movement to include the community ownership of entire villages. In moving toward his goal of 50 million acres, by 1960 he had obtained 4,411,191 acres of land and 4,643 villages and had distributed 872,609 acres.

One great hope for accelerating rural progress was the Community Development Program launched in 1952 in fifty-five separate areas. The object was "to develop self-reliance in the individual and initiative in the village community." Technical and financial assistance was offered by the central government, priority being given once again to increasing agricultural output. Communications, education, housing, health, sanitation, welfare, and small-scale industry are emphasized. As of 1957 it was felt that the plan had failed, since the people were not representing themselves; insufficient local interest or initiative had been evoked.

In 1959 the Community Development concept was broadened to include the concept of government by village councils. Thus power, resources, and responsibility are delegated to the "grass roots" level to implement development. The *panchayat,* or village council, is elected and entitled to a share of land revenue. In turn it levies taxes and receives income from local enterprises. The emphasis, then, has been shifted toward self-help. Nevertheless change is slow in rural areas where people cling to superstition and tradition. But there seems to be hope even for these areas, though more rapid change is needed to meet increasing demands for food.

Industry

Possessing one of the largest iron ore reserves in the world, India now has five major steel plants, with a total capacity of six million tons. Ninety per cent of the bituminous coal and most of the iron are located in the northeastern area of the country. Bauxite deposits are also large. Huge textile mills are situated around Madras, Calcutta, and Bombay. Prior to the partition in 1947 India was the world's second largest producer of cotton, but her production was cut in half when Pakistan received much of the cotton-producing area. Official Indian sources report that 6.5 million non-agricultural workers entered the field of industry between 1955 and 1961, with 10.5 million more expected by 1966.

Industrial progress has been tremendous since independence. Although many private enterprises continue to flourish, public utilities and most basic industries with few exceptions are state owned. Incentives in the form of loans, buildings, and technical assistance have been offered by the government to small-scale industries. This has resulted in increased production of such light consumer goods as plastics, bicycles, and sewing machines. India still faces many critical problems in the industrial sectors: transportation facilities must be expanded to meet increased industrial demands; exploitation of vital resources must meet demands; training of sufficient managerial and technical personnel is necessary; an entrepreneurial class with investment skill must replace the traditional short-term trader-merchant; and the civil bureaucracy must be kept to a minimum.

India lacks a favorable balance of trade because many expensive imports, such as machinery, petroleum, and food products, are paid for in such relatively inexpensive Indian exports as tea (the main cash crop), rubber, jute, leather, hides, and textiles. With the assistance of foreign aid India is managing to survive on an austerity basis.

Economic Planning

Since gaining independence India has launched three five-year plans. The first plan, covering the period 1951–56, called for a total outlay of $4.3 billion. The main target of the plan was to increase agricultural production, and it gave priority to land reform and rural development programs. While continuing to invest in the agricultural, transportation, and communication sectors, the second Indian five-year plan (1956–61) provided increased outlays to basic and heavy industry, with an overall outlay of $10 billion. The third plan (1961–66) calls for $15 billion from public funds and $9 billion from private sectors. Industry and mining will receive about 20 per cent; agriculture, irrigation, and community development 23 per cent; transportation 20 per cent; and social services about 17 per cent. Attention is still focused on agriculture, since the rate of growth in this area seems to be one of the main factors limiting over-all economic programs. At the same time that efforts are being made to increase agricultural output, rural economies are being diversified and that proportion of the entire economy dependent on agriculture is being reduced.

India's economic programs represent the largest scale of planned development in a democratic state. Intensive five-year plans are to continue until 1976. With 1949–50 as the base year of 100, it has been estimated that agricultural production had increased to 141 by 1960–61. Industrial production rose to 194 from 1950–51 as the base year. National income increased 42 per cent, school enrollment 85 per cent, and income per capita from $59.64 a year to $69.30.

These statistics mean little when one reflects on India's biggest problem—population growth. At the rate of 2.2 per cent increase a year the population estimate for 1986 is 625 million. This led Dr. C. Chandrasekaron, director of the Demographic Training and

Research Center of Bombay, to comment that the increase in food production and national income achieved during the two five-year plans has hardly led to any appreciable improvement in the living standards of the people. The stabilization of population growth, then, has become the very center of development planning, with about $100 million being allocated for birth control in the third five-year plan. At the same time the Indian government has emphasized that food production still has top priority, since family planning will not solve the problem of feeding the existing millions. Therefore among the goals of the third plan is India's hope to achieve self-sufficiency in grain production. If industrial growth can be expanded at the same time, perhaps in a decade India can rely mainly on domestic resources instead of on external aid. It is hoped that national income will increase by more than 5 per cent annually and income per capita will be 17 per cent greater by 1966. Expanded educational facilities would be available to all Indians from 6 to 11 years old. But to reach these goals means greater tax burdens, greater austerity for an already deprived people.

The third plan calls for $5.733 billion in foreign aid. A consortium of the International Bank for Reconstruction and Development with large United States contributions will supply the necessary aid. Likewise India hopes to attract approximately $630 million in private foreign investment.

Prospects for Development

On the whole, India's developmental prospects look good. Of all the newly independent countries India appears to have the best chance of attaining the status of a true political democracy—a regime of civilian rule through representative institutions with public liberties. The keys to this conclusion are to be found in India's capable leadership, smooth-running civil service, high-caliber army, and rapidly increasing politically conscious electorate.

India's economic prospects are less sanguine. Agricultural production has risen since 1950 by 25 per cent, but this rate barely balances the huge increase in population. In industry, steel output in the last decade rose by 25 per cent, coal by 33 per cent, cement by 100 per cent, electric power by 150 per cent, and fertilizer production by 900 per cent. But the industrial sector is still so small that its impact on total growth is limited. From 1950 to 1958 India's gross national product rose but 30 per cent in real terms, or—at best —only 1.5 per cent per year faster than population growth. It is hoped that as village isolation breaks down, as social mobility increases, as the impact of the five-year plans takes effect, a second industrial revolution will occur. If the West can promote Indian economic stability to a sufficient degree, hopefully a program of technological and economic assistance can help India achieve an industrial "take-off."

Unsolved foreign policy problems still persist. Continuing bad relations with Pakistan over Kashmir, aggravated by the Rann de Kutch incident, and unsettled relations with Communist China pose major question marks for India's future development. The minor Sino-Indian border war of 1962 and the military effort associated with it had a significant impact upon national economic planning by diverting scarce resources to war purposes. A repetition of this incident or a major crisis in Kashmir could have a similar negative effect. Despite these foreign policy and economic problems, India is the most stable and influential of the emerging nations, and because of her importance in the future of the world the technologically advanced nations of the Western world will undoubtedly continue to aid her economic developmental processes.

SELECTED BIBLIOGRAPHY

BROWN, W. N. *The United States and India and Pakistan.* Rev. edn. Cambridge, Mass.: Harvard Univ. Press, 1963.

EPSTEIN, T. S. *Economic Development and Social Change in South India.* Manchester, Eng.: Manchester Univ. Press, 1962.

HARRISON, S. S. *India: The Most Dangerous Decade.* Princeton, N.J.: Princeton Univ. Press, 1960.

HARRISON, S. S., ed. *India and the United States.* New York: Macmillan, 1961.

LAMB, B. P. *India: A World in Transition.* New York: Praeger, 1963.

LEWIS, J. P. *Quiet Crisis in India.* Washington, D.C.: The Brookings Institution, 1962.

PALMER, N. D. *The Indian Political System.* Boston: Houghton Mifflin, 1961.

PARK, R. L., ed. *Leadership and Political Institutions in India.* Princeton, N.J.: Princeton Univ. Press, 1959.

PHILIPS, C. H., ed. *Politics and Society in India.* New York: Praeger, 1962.

SPEAR, PERCIVAL, ed. *Oxford History of India.* Rev. edn. London: Oxford Univ. Press, 1961.

Pakistan

In August 1947 India received its independence from Great Britain. At that same time Pakistan was created from territories originally part of India but largely inhabited by Moslems. The fundamental objective in creating Pakistan was to provide a place for the Moslem people of the subcontinent to live and preserve their religion, culture, and particular way of life. Pakistan has a population of approximately 100 million, with an annual rate of growth of 2.2 per cent. The nation is divided into two parts that are separated by a distance of nearly one thousand miles. West Pakistan, a waterless, barren, and sparsely populated region, has an area of approximately 310,000 square miles and lies on both sides of the Indus River. By contrast East Pakistan is a compact, densely populated area of approximately 34,501 square miles. Created from the old province of Bengal and a small part of Assam, East Pakistan enjoys a warm, rainy climate and a relatively fertile soil, but it is overcrowded. More than 85 per cent of Pakistanis are illiterate and unskilled. Income per capita averages $72 annually, and poverty is an almost universal condition. The average landholding is about 0.6 acre. Pakistan is now running a balance of payments deficit of approximately $240 million annually, which is compensated for only by foreign aid from the United States and other international sources.

National Unity and Ideology

Pakistan was born of what was really a revolutionary movement within a state—the Moslem League, founded in India in 1906. At Independence in 1947 its leaders faced an ideological vacuum. Percival Spear analyzes the situation as follows: "As Pakistan settled

184

down *it was gradually realized that there was no solid basis for the new state.* There was an overriding fear; there were conflicting deep-seated feelings which were potential forces; there were rival theories which divided and bemused the leaders."[1] The fear was of the Indian Hindus—originally fear of absorption into Hinduism as the prospect of Indian self-government grew and now fear of the superior strength of India. As for the conflicting, deep-seated feelings, one must include the Islamic faith itself, which is split into many sects and heresies, as well as the very powerful force of provincialism. The dissonance is not only between East and West Pakistan, but regional feeling is strong within West Pakistan itself. What of the "rival theories"? Democracy was one, and a rallying cry of the Western-educated intelligentsia. The views of the orthodox Islamic doctors who oppose Western innovations in the sphere of women's rights and the position of non-Moslems in the state constituted another. The Moslem modernists who tried to build a bridge between the two other groups were a third force.[2]

If it be conceded that there are no firm foundations for a modern state in Pakistan, what are the cohesive elements which have enabled it to survive? Spear enumerates four: (1) the Islamic sentiment in its broadest sense, (2) anti-Indian sentiment, (3) the general respect for authority in Pakistan, as in Moslem communities in general, and (4) the widespread desire in Pakistan to get on terms with or be level with the West.[3]

Political Development

Pakistan's political history since independence has been largely a history of successive autocrats. Mohammed Ali Jinnah, the "father of Pakistan," served as governor-general from August 1947 until his death in September 1948. He was far more than a ceremonial head of state and exercised what was in effect a kind of dictatorship. Jinnah was succeeded by a series of well-intentioned but ineffective

---

[1] Percival Spear, "The Political Evolution of Pakistan," in *Politics in Southern Asia*, ed. Saul Rose (New York: St. Martin's Press, 1963), p. 37.
[2] Ibid., p. 38. [3] Ibid., p. 39.

political leaders—Nazimuddin, Ghulam Mohammed, and Mirza. In desperation, Mirza abrogated the Constitution on October 7, 1958, and invited the army to take power. On October 27 it did so, and General Ayub Khan, commander-in-chief of the army, assumed the presidency, which he has held ever since.

From independence until the military coup in October 1958 Pakistan operated under a constituent assembly, which originally was the Pakistani portion of the assembly created in undivided India prior to partition. Upon the ruling of the Pakistan federal court, a new constituent assembly was created and convened in July 1955. A constitution was promulgated in March 1956 but abrogated in October 1958. On June 12, 1959, President Khan's revolutionary government announced the establishment of a system of representative government known as "basic democracies." This concept has now been incorporated into the new constitution of March 1, 1962, under which Pakistan elected a national assembly in April 1962 and provincial assemblies on May 6, 1962.

The Khan plan proceeded from the premise that a democratic parliamentary government based on the British model was not feasible in Pakistan because of the widespread illiteracy and poverty. Accordingly he proposed a five-level political system starting at the bottom and working upwards. It consists of (1) union councils, or town committees, (2) subdivisional or *Tehsil* councils, (3) district councils, (4) divisional councils, and (5) provincial advisory development councils (one for East and one for West Pakistan). At every level membership is partly elective and partly appointive. At the first or grass-roots level of the system each wing of Pakistan is divided into forty thousand constituencies with an average population of about one thousand each. Each constituency elects one representative by universal adult suffrage who is designated an elector. Ten of such electors, together with five members appointed by the central government, form the union council, or town committee. These eighty thousand electors also elect the president and the 156 members of the unicameral national assembly, as well as the two provincial assemblies of 155 members each. Otherwise the structure of the government is the federal form with a president. The president is not responsible to the legislature, and political parties are prohibited. The president has the power of veto over legislation and the power of dissolving the assembly. He appoints both ministers and governors of the provinces. The judiciary is independent. There is a list of subjects over which the central legislature has control. All other subjects are left to the provinces.

Although this constitution has its critics, it has much to be said in its favor. It recognizes the pre-eminent role of authority in Moslem societies. At the same time it provides a channel of communication by which the ruling authority both consults and is influenced by the people at the grass-roots level. The weakness of this government is its provisional character and the narrow base of its support. However as a transitory regime promoting an incipient tutelary democracy the military clearly provides the best short-run alternative, particularly in contrast to the other available elite groups —the corrupt politicians, the landlords, and the *Ulema* (Moslem theologians). What Pakistan needs in the long run, however, is a dynamic, political elite group that is able to maintain itself and draw strength from the whole society—a hybrid, perhaps, of the Communist party in the Soviet Union and the Congress party in India.

A presidential election was held on January 2, 1965. Ayub Khan, who had quietly seized power in 1958, presented himself in a free election. His opponent was no obscurity—none other than Fatimah Jinnah, sister of the late Mohammed Ali Jinnah, who had led Pakistan's fight for independence. She had the support of five of the old political parties which Ayub had suppressed in his 1958 coup. Ayub won the election by approximately 50,000 votes to Miss Jinnah's 28,000. Although his opponents were surprised, the result was not unexpected. In a nation where true democracy is unknown, Ayub's tutelary brand has enjoyed more than limited success. Under Ayub "Pakistan has prospered as never before. A certain amount of inflation has inevitably accompanied rapid industrial expansion, but price rises are modest compared with those of India. Last year's grain harvest and such cash crops as jute were excellent: the farmers are doing well. The country is receiving roughly a million dollars a day in economic aid, not to mention military assistance, practically all of it from the United States—American business has not been deterred from steadily increasing its investment in Pakistan."[4] Relative prosperity is thus the key to Pakistan's current political stability.

Economic Development

Similar to that of most underdeveloped countries, Pakistan's economy is basically agricultural. The principal food crops for consumption are wheat and rice, while cotton and jute are grown for export purposes. Methods of cultivation are primitive, and productivity is extremely low. Pakistan has few natural resources and is further handicapped by the uneconomic division of the country into two widely separated provinces. As a result Pakistan is unable to sustain itself on its own resources. Suffering a chronic food deficit, Pakistan is heavily dependent on grain imports from the United States.

Since partition in 1947 some industry has developed. Cotton textiles, jute goods, and electrical products are Pakistan's principal manufactures. In general, however, Pakistan's industrial development has been retarded by such interrelated factors as the low level of literacy and the lack of trained manpower and entrepreneurial skills. These factors along with the stubborn persistence of unfavorable social attitudes have resulted in a great deal of inefficiency in both industry and commerce. Pakistan's export earnings are insufficient to finance the importation of goods necessary for sustaining the economy as well as for development. As a result Pakistan can satisfy its balance of payments deficit only through foreign aid.

For the first eight years of independence Pakistan's economic development was chaotic and uneven. In 1955 Pakistan launched its first five-year plan. Under this plan a total of $2.8 billion was expended, with priority given to investment in irrigation, power, and industry. Industrial production and infrastructure facilities expanded significantly. Inflation was brought under control, land reform was extended, and corruption was reduced. But insufficient attention was given to agriculture. An effort to remedy this defi-

[4] *The Reporter*, February 11, 1965, pp. 34–36.

ciency is now being made through the second five-year plan, under-way since 1960.

The second five-year plan calls for expenditures of $4.8 billion. Over the full period of the plan it is estimated that the gross national product will increase by 24 per cent, resulting from increases of 14 per cent and 15 per cent in agricultural and industrial output. Income per capita is expected to rise 2.5 per cent annually, the number of children attending primary schools is to rise to 60 per cent, malaria is to be eradicated, self-sufficiency in food grains is to be achieved, and a 25 per cent increase in electric power capacity is planned. This massive program of economic growth is to be financed by an international consortium plus $722 million in surplus wheat shipments from the United States.

With a 2.2 per cent annual growth in population and an ex-tremely high density of population, Pakistan must launch an attack on the birth rate. Under the first five-year plan only some pilot work was undertaken. The second five-year plan is more aggressive on the subject and seeks to provide the necessary medical and other facilities as well as to influence social attitudes and practices in favor of family planning.

Developmental Prospects

Realistically speaking, Pakistan's developmental prospects are only fair. Temporarily, at least, Ayub Khan and the military have restored political stability, thus bringing some semblance of order to a nation beset with political corruption, sectionalism, and severe inflation. As a transitory regime the Khan government offers a breathing space, but will it be long enough? Created out of a revolutionary void, Pakistan lacks cohesion—geographically, ideo-logically, and economically. Its people do not speak a uniform language, and many are illiterate. There is still no real sense of nationhood in the country, which is united only in its hatred of Hindu India. It is a nation divided in two—physically, mentally, and culturally. Pakistan's economic problems are serious. Lacking natural resources and a favorable climate, it is faced with the omni-present threat of famine. While much effort already has and is still being expended to deal with agricultural problems, gains in this area tend to be swallowed up by the rapidly expanding population.

On the favorable side there has been marked progress under the second five-year plan. In 1963 the rate of the gross national product increased 5 per cent. In line with the government's policy of priority to heavy industry, industrial growth is being aggressively fostered and plans for the construction of two steel mills are underway. Note, however, that this has been largely due to massive infusions of foreign economic assistance, principally from the United States and through the World Bank.

Still ominously threatening both India and Pakistan is the problem of their ability to coexist. While a compromise solution was found concerning the use of the waters of the Indus River basin, the explosive Kashmir question remains unsettled. Although the Rann of Kutch Incident (concerning a mutually contiguous wasteland thought to contain oil) has now apparently been settled by a truce with India, Pakistan still faces border difficulties with Afghanistan. Thus the developmental prospects of Pakistan are dependent on a long series of uncertain contingencies—its ability to avoid war with its neighbors, its political stability, its agricultural and industrial growth, and its population problem.

SELECTED BIBLIOGRAPHY

ANDRUS, J. R., and A. F. MOHAMMUD. *The Economy of Pakistan.* London: Oxford Univ. Press, 1958.

BINDER, LEONARD. *Religion and Politics in Pakistan.* Berkeley: Univ. of California Press, 1961.

BROWN, W. N. *The United States and India and Pakistan.* 2nd edn. Cambridge, Mass.: Harvard Univ. Press, 1963.

CALLARD, K. B. *Pakistan: A Political Study.* New York: Macmillan, 1960.

———. *Political Forces in Pakistan, 1947–1959.* Vancouver: Institute of Pacific Relations, 1959.

PEACH, W. N., MOHAMMED UZAIR, and G. W. RUCKER. *Basic Data of the Economy of Pakistan.* Karachi: Oxford Univ. Press, 1959.

SIDDIGI, ASLAM, *Pakistan Seeks Security.* Lahore: Longmans, Green and Co., 1960.

SYMONDS, RICHARD. *The Making of Pakistan.* London: Faber and Faber, 1959.

Indonesia

The Republic of Indonesia is the largest and most populous nation in Southeast Asia. It is potentially the most powerful. It is the world's largest archipelago, and it extends for more than three thousand miles along the equator, strategically placed between the southeast Asian mainland and the continent of Australia. It consists of six main islands—Sumatra, Java, Kalimantan, Celebes, Nusa, Tenggara, the Moluccas—and more than three thousand smaller islands. Its population now numbers more than one hundred million and includes a variety of races: Javanese, Sudanese, Madurese, Achinese, Bataks, and Minangkabus are the principal ethnic components of the nation. Ninety per cent of Indonesians are Moslem. Potentially Indonesia is one of the richest nations in the world with respect to natural resources. It possesses large reserves of tin, oil, and coal, as well as ample deposits of manganese, bauxite, copper, nickel, silver, and gold. In addition its rich, volcanic soil permits an agriculture-centered population to produce rubber, rice, copra, maize, tobacco, coffee, sugar, casava, and indigo.

The Dutch East India Company ruled Indonesia for almost two centuries from 1602 to 1798. Indirect rule was employed, whereby local rulers and chieftains continued to govern but were in fact puppets of the exploiting country. In 1798 the Company was officially disbanded, and its functions were assumed by the Dutch government itself. In the early part of the nineteenth century the British seized and held the archipelago for four years. The Dutch returned in 1816, and in 1830 they inaugurated a new program of extensive forced cultivation which was known as the "culture system." Under this system the peasants were required to plant one fifth of their land for designated export crops and to work for 66 days each year on government plantations. As a result great improvements in agricultural production took place—crop rotation was introduced, irrigation and communications facilities were improved, pest control campaigns were launched. Spectacular increases in both crops and population resulted. The culture system was eventually abolished, and control of cultivation passed to private contractors, who were primarily resident Chinese. Thus development created a growing number of landless peasants. During the nineteenth century recurrent but uncoordinated rebel uprisings were ruthlessly suppressed.

In 1901, the so-called "ethical policy" was adopted. This new policy, although extremely paternalistic in character, did nevertheless provide for both expanded social welfare services and the improvement of the infrastructure of the country. Under this policy roads were built, plans for soil development and conservation were initiated, agricultural and fishery production was expanded, and education was provided for a select minority. The Dutch thus trained an intellectual elite who later became nationalists and revolutionary leaders. What they failed to do was to train a corps of administrators, businessmen, and professional men who were even remotely adequate to the needs of the nation.

National Unity and Ideology

A strong sense of national unity is lacking in Indonesia. This situation is due not only to the vastness of the country but more particularly to significant disparities between the islands with respect to population and natural resources. Java, for example, the center of Indonesian government, is densely populated, packing some 66 million inhabitants into 9 per cent of the nation's land area. Sumatra, on the other hand, has only 16 per cent of the nation's population and 32 per cent of the land area, but it produces 70 per cent of the nation's exports. Kalimantan—Indonesia's part of Borneo—is a vast equatorial wasteland with only a scattering of tribesmen and oil installations. The result of these disparities has been a series of secessionist movements in the so-called "outer islands" against the central government in Java. In 1958 guerrilla resistance erupted on both Sumatra and the Celebes, and 50 per cent of the government's annual budget was consumed in the necessary warfare campaigns. Since the central government has still failed to satisfy the demands of these outer islands for both a degree of governmental autonomy and a fair share of the national income, regional dissidence will continue to be a serious problem for Indonesia.

The official ideology of Indonesia was developed by President Sukarno in 1927. It is called *Marhaenism,* which he described as "Indonesian Marxism." In 1945 Sukarno adjusted Marhaenism to the new world order by proposing the "five principles" of the new Indonesian nation: nationalism, internationalism, democracy, social justice, and belief in God. Following the vicissitudes of the post-independence years, Sukarno proposed a further refinement—a "way out" of Indonesian crises. This concept was codified in 1959 as USDEK, which stands for the 1945 constitution, Indonesian socialism, guided democracy, guided economy, and Indonesian identity. To sophisticated Westerners all of these slogans seem nothing more than shibboleths. To the unsophisticated masses of Indonesia they undoubtedly provide useful rallying cries and serve the same purpose as phrases such as "the American way of life" and the "free enterprise system."

Political Development

Indonesian nationalism dates from the early 1900s. The Dutch-trained intellectual elite banded together in self-improvement societies which rapidly acquired political overtones. In 1908 the Budi Utomo (Beautiful Endeavor), a union of railway workers, was established. In 1911 the Serikat Islam was founded. Originally a religious and trade league, the Islam was the mother of all modern Indonesian political parties. It survived in a unified form until 1923, when it splintered into three major factions. The Marxists, after unsuccessfully attempting to usurp control, split off to form the PKI, the oldest Communist party in Southeast Asia. The Moslems turned more toward religious revival and became the Masjumi party of today. The third group, including President Sukarno, formed the PNI (Nationalist Party of Indonesia) in 1927 and assumed primary leadership of the nationalist movement.

During the 1930s Dutch colonial policy became extremely

repressive. Both the PKI and the PNI were dissolved, and both Communist and nationalist leaders went either to jail or into exile. Indonesian nationalism, however, did not receive any encouragement until the Japanese occupation during World War II. The Japanese—for their own purposes—encouraged nationalist movements throughout Southeast Asia. This was the making of these movements, especially that in Indonesia. In Indonesia not only was the movement encouraged, but many nationalists were freed from prison. The Dutch language was officially banned, giving encouragement to the use of the native tongue. The government was purged of all Dutch officials, which not only created many positions for the natives but also made available much-needed training in administrative skills. Finally, during the occupation the Japanese created an Indonesian army, which hitherto had not existed.

Thus Indonesia was able to declare its independence two days after the local Japanese surrender on April 17, 1945. It was the first former colony in Southeast Asia to do so. An independent Indonesian republic was proclaimed with Sukarno as president and Mohammed Hatta as vice-president. It lasted for approximately six weeks—until the return of the Dutch. Firmly convinced that these "childlike" natives could not function without kind but firm paternalism, the Dutch dedicated themselves for the next four years to the recovery of the colony. During this period countless negotiations took place; legalistic statements of settlement which were outmoded by the time they had been sealed were issued; and blitzkrieg attacks were launched by the Dutch on nationalist strongholds in the cities. By the end of 1947 world indignation was aroused by the Dutch strong-arm tactics in Indonesia, and pressure by both the United States and the United Nations eventually forced the Dutch to accede to Indonesian independence. On November 2, 1949, sovereignty was transferred over all Indonesia except Netherlands New Guinea (West Irian) to the Republic of the United States of Indonesia, a federal state.

Within seven months after independence the member states of the Indonesian republic dismantled their federation and created a highly centralized unitary state with what has since been known as the constitution of 1950. Local leaders lost their power to provincial governors appointed from Djakarta. The president was confirmed in office, but his ministers were no longer responsible to him, but to a multiparty parliament. In this parliament there were thirty leading political parties and three principal groups. The largest and most loosely organized was and is the Masjumi (Moslem) party, which was dominated by the "religious socialists," who reconciled modern Islamic ideals with socialism and who saw the need for economic and political cooperation with the West. The PKI (Communist) party was and is a tight-knit, well-organized, and disciplined party with good leadership and an efficient organization in the trade unions and among the peasants. Between the Moslem party and the Communist party stood the PNI—the Indonesian Nationalist party. Its membership was drawn largely from the civil service and the new commercial and professional classes. It was and is the most blatantly nationalist group, and its greatest asset is its association with the personal influence of President Sukarno.

No one party held more than 20 per cent of the seats in Parliament, so party groupings were unstable, and short-lived coalition governments were the rule. As a result there were five cabinets during the period 1950–55, none of which was able to come to grips with the fundamental problems of the country—demobilization, internal security, and the balance of payments situation. The failures of these coalition governments were due not only to their instability but also to political intrigue by the president himself.

New elections were held in 1955, but the new coalition cabinet which emerged was more ineffective than those preceding it. President Sukarno became more and more frustrated by the operation of the party system. On March 14, 1957, the last parliamentary cabinet resigned, and Sukarno proclaimed a nationwide state of war and siege and assumed full powers as president and commander-in-chief. A rebel provisional government was established in Central Sumatra in February 1958. It demanded greater autonomy, the return of Mohammed Hatta (a moderate) to the government, and the elimination of Communist influence from the government. Sukarno ignored these demands and ordered the rebellion suppressed. It eventually was.

In 1959, Sukarno secured the abolition of the 1950 constitution and a return to the wartime 1945 constitution under which he enjoyed far wider powers—for example, the right to make laws with the agreement of Parliament, except during a state of emergency, when he was empowered to act alone. In 1960 he created a new parliamentary institution—the Gotong-Royong (Mutual Cooperation) Parliament. This unicameral representative group includes both members of "approved" political parties (PNI, Moslem Teachers, and the Communists) and representatives in equal proportions from functional groups—labor, armed forces, peasants, religious groups, women's organizations, and so on. Sukarno calls this new system "guided democracy." He utilizes the tutelary system by skillfully balancing off the army, admittedly the strongest power center in the nation, against the Communist party, which with the dissolution of the parliament has become the strongest political party. It is, however, a precarious equilibrium.

Unfortunately, Sukarno has been more concerned with international affairs than domestic problems. The result is that the Indonesian economy has deteriorated very badly. It was hoped that he would be satisfied to secure West Irian (West New Guinea). Upon the formation of Malaysia in September 1963 he has turned his attention to a "crush Malaysia" program. In part this approach represents a diversionary attempt to turn the eyes of his people away from a mounting domestic crisis. Sadly, however, such an approach exacerbated the continuing economic crisis.

Economic Development

The Indonesian economic picture is frightful and tragic—tragic in that this naturally rich country is not far from a state of economic collapse. Were it not for the relative self-sufficiency of the peasants, who constitute 80 per cent of the population, the economy would probably have collapsed already.

Indonesian exports in both volume and value are less now than they were ten years ago. Except for oil all of Indonesia's major exports are running far below the prewar level. Rubber, the principal export and mainstay of the economy, declined 10 per cent in value of exports during the period 1950–60 and continues to decline. Rice, another previously vital export, has risen only 10 per cent in production, while the population has increased by 30 per cent since World War II. Indonesia, once a major exporter of rice, now imports it.

On the industrial side Indonesia is also in serious plight. In recent years industry has been functioning at only 50–60 per cent of capacity, primarily because of a shortage of spare parts and raw materials. And inflation has also been accentuated by governmental budgets totally lacking in adequate governmental investment in economic development. Although private foreign investment has been discouraged, the ratio of government investment to government expenditure is very low. The already serious inflation was further stimulated during the 1958–61 rebellion and during the Irian campaign when 50 per cent of the government's budget was for military expenditures. Increasing inflation has brought about rampant speculation and the hoarding of scarce commodities, a situation which has stifled industrial growth and hampered effective economic planning.

Seemingly, the *coup de grace* to the Indonesian economy is the "crush Malaysia" campaign. Not only has the campaign cost the country heavily in terms of military expenditures, but Indonesia's economic embargo of the newly formed Federation of Malaysia is economically absurd, since Malaysia is the major market for Indonesia's exports. The federation itself absorbs some 52 per cent of the total annual exports of Indonesia ($674 million) while the majority of Indonesia's shipping uses the Malaysian ports of Singapore and Penang. In addition only Singapore has the necessary facilities for processing the low grades of the Indonesian rubber crop.

Indonesia's militant position toward Malaysia has also resulted in the termination of U.S. economic aid vitally needed by the floundering country. The United States not only withdrew its support from a multinational, $250 million stabilization program intended to help balance Indonesia's large trade deficit, but it also discontinued all direct economic aid to Indonesia. Thus at present only a bleak future and a fateful day of reckoning for the Indonesian economy can be seen.

A major cause of the disaster has been governmental mismanagement. The dismantling of the capitalist-colonialist inheritance was successfully carried out by Sukarno and his colleagues, while the development of a planned economy to replace it has been a complete failure. The bureaucracy itself has drifted toward exploitation. Meanwhile the lack of economic discipline has produced governmental economic policies with vast utopian goals but without the practical administrative procedures necessary to produce even short-run successes.

Income per capita is declining; industry and commerce are stagnating; the population continues to grow at a rate of 2.1 per cent. This latter problem is especially troubling. Despite population projections that Indonesia will have an estimated population of 150 million by 1983, the government takes the stand that the problem is not one of overpopulation but of maldistribution of population. It refuses to promote family planning measures. Meanwhile its only approach to the problem—migration—has bogged down in administrative confusion and the psychological difficulties of persuading those from the overpopulated islands to leave home and persuading their proposed new homes to accept them.

Developmental Prospects

The short-term developmental prospects for Indonesia appear bleak. President Sukarno, although not an able administrator, seems nevertheless to possess sufficient charisma and tactical political skill to keep himself in power. But with the continuing deterioration of the Indonesian economy a day of reckoning is approaching. Earlier speculation centered upon Army Chief of Staff Nasution as Sukarno's probable successor, when and if he falls from power or dies. More recent political developments in Indonesia have cast considerable doubt upon this possibility. Current speculation tends to focus on Foreign Minister Subandrio as the likely successor. Subandrio's potential power rests upon the support of the PKI. Nasution's power base is, of course, the army. At present (June 1965) Subandrio seems also to have managed by means of servility and political skill to obtain Sukarno's blessing, which would tip the scales in his favor. If Nasution were nevertheless to emerge as the successor and were to play a national modernizing role in Indonesia comparable to that played by President Nasser in Egypt or President Khan in Pakistan, the Indonesian political picture would be considerably brighter. A more likely Subandrio succession would be bad news. At best he would juggle precariously between the PKI and the PNI. At worst he might become a PKI puppet. And worse still, a covert or overt grab for exclusive power by the PKI, with or without Sukarno, would probably precipitate a civil war by the military as a desperate countermeasure. Indonesia's political future is not promising.

Given its great economic potential, Indonesia could, with international assistance, set its economic house in order. This was the hope underlying the very promising $250 million international consortium formed in early 1963—to stabilize Indonesia's economy until much needed self-help, austerity, and stabilization measures could take effect. This opportunity was lost once the "crush Malaysia" campaign had been launched. Although this policy of "irresponsible adventurism" is not succeeding, there are no signs that President Sukarno intends to desist from it. Consequently as the economy continues to deteriorate, the immediate economic prospects for the country are very dim. It might well be inquired whether or not the economic crisis will soon become sufficiently acute to force Sukarno's hand, making him agree to some new stabilization program. Unfortunately his past successes both in suppressing local revolts and in securing West Irian suggest that he is likely to gamble on continued success rather than face up to his domestic problems in a resolute manner. But how long will Nasution and the military permit Sukarno to gamble Micawber-like that "something will turn up"?

In the long run a more rational approach to Indonesia's domestic problems is inevitable. The military budget must be reduced and the army converted into a compact, efficient, and professional body. A compromise solution must be worked out between the central government and the outer islands not only in regard to sharing revenue but also to providing these areas with some measure of autonomy. The major nationalization must take place in the economy itself. Foreign investment must be encouraged. Inflation and tax evasion by smuggling must be curbed. A mushrooming bureaucracy must be pruned and reorganized. A new national economic plan, adequate and appropriate for Indonesia's high priority needs, must be developed.

Fortunately, as a result of foreign economic assistance, great improvements have been made in Indonesia's public health and public education programs. The nation is moving toward universal free primary education, and it is also taking steps through adult education to develop a literate adult majority. Future population pressures, however, hang heavily over the nation and must eventually be dealt with.

SELECTED BIBLIOGRAPHY

BRACKMAN, A. C. *Indonesian Communism: A History.* New York: Praeger, 1963.

FEITH, HERBERT. *The Decline of Constitutional Democracy in Indonesia.* Ithaca, N.Y.: Cornell Univ. Press, 1962.

FISCHER, LOUIS. *The Story of Indonesia.* New York: Harper, 1959.

HANNA, W. A. *Bung Karno's Indonesia.* Rev. edn. New York: American Univ. Field Staff, 1961.

KAHIN, G. MC T. *Nationalism and Revolution in Indonesia.* Ithaca, N.Y.: Cornell Univ. Press, 1952.

———. "Indonesia," in *Major Governments of Asia,* ed. G. McT. Kahin. 2d edn. Ithaca, N.Y.: Cornell Univ. Press, 1963.

MC VEY, R. T., ed. *Indonesia.* New Haven, Conn.: Human Relations Area Files, Inc., 1963.

MINTZ, J. S. *Indonesia: A Profile.* Princeton, N.J.: Van Nostrand, 1961.

———. *Mohammed, Marx and Marhaen: The Roots of Indonesian Socialism.* New York: Praeger, 1965.

PARKER, GUY J. "The Role of the Military in Indonesia," in *The Military in the Underdeveloped Areas,* ed. J. J. Johnson. Princeton, N.J.: Princeton Univ. Press, 1962.

SOEDJATNOKO. "The Role of Political Parties in Indonesia," in *Nationalism and Progress in Free Asia,* ed. P. W. Thayer. Baltimore: Johns Hopkins Press, 1956.

Thailand

With an estimated population of 30 million, the kingdom of Thailand is the central and most populous country on the mainland of Southeast Asia. Its total area is approximately 200,000 square miles, a little less than that of Texas. Of all the countries in the region Thailand alone escaped a period of Western colonial rule. Thailand has a diversified topography and a monsoon climate—tropical with high temperatures and humidity and with marked seasonal variations. Its land mass is dominated by a central alluvial plain, bounded by a system of mountain ranges and the great Mekong River. It has in general a rich and fertile soil, resulting in a favorable balance of population to resources. Agriculture is the primary basis of life, and the Thai social structure is characterized by a sharp division into two main classes—an aristocracy and a rural peasantry—which have a common tie in the Buddhist religion. The population of Thailand is basically homogeneous, but there are three principal minority groups: (1) three million ethnic Chinese who dominate the commerce of the country, (2) 700,000 Malays who are Moslems and are concentrated in the southern peninsula, and (3) 30,000 Vietnamese. Thai is the common language of the nation, but English is widely spoken and understood by the official, commercial, and educated classes.

National Unity and Ideology

Thailand is a very stable, conservative state. National unity has been sought after as the chief political objective for several hundred years. This theme can be traced even in the historical inscriptions and in the literary epics of the medieval period. In part this unity has been sought as a means of avoiding fatal disunity in a climate of increasing foreign pressure. It is also explained by the fact that Thailand has managed to maintain its political independence during a long period of colonial rule on all sides.

The present Thai dynasty was established in 1782, and it has since then produced several great and able kings who yielded where necessary but who also consolidated and reorganized what remained. In addition the ruling oligarchy has over the years remained a remarkably cohesive force. The combination produced a strong, centralized government which has not only maintained the country's independence but has slowly adapted to the demands of the modern world. By and large the Thai people are happy and well fed and do not feel oppressed. Consequently Thailand possesses a highly developed sense of national unity. The only exceptions to this generalization are the undigested minority groups—the Chinese, Malays, and Vietnamese—and the poverty-stricken people in the northeast, many of whom are ethnically Lao and have traditionally felt a sense of remoteness and alienation from the central government.

There is really no national ideology in Thailand other than the predominant national religion of Buddhism. The absence of a colonizing power inhibited the rise of a militant anti-Western nationalism. What concerns there have been about Thai frontiers, for example, have been a "pro-Thai" rather than an anti-Western nationalism—a politician's nationalism, as it were. Communism appears to have had little appeal to the Thais, and, except in the northeast, there are no significant evidences of Communist subversion. On the other hand genuine democratic liberalism has enjoyed little success other than in a superficial sense. In 1932 the Thais adopted the trappings of parliamentary democracy, but they have practiced the realities of the system only during brief, unsuccessful "trial periods" when political parties were permitted to operate. Nevertheless this conservative political amalgam provides the Thai state with a great deal of stability, which is no small asset for a developing society. In fact this situation would appear on balance to be a very favorable omen for future Thai development, since the nature of the Thai people is also to be receptive and flexible, to accept change gradually, and to be adaptive.

Political Development

Since the constitutional revolution of 1932 Thailand has nominally been a constitutional monarchy possessing most of the superficial indicia of a parliamentary government. Actually, however, with the exception of three brief periods in 1932–33, 1946–47, and 1954–57, Thailand has been nothing more than a military oligarchy with governmental changes taking place as a result of relatively bloodless internal shifts of power.

On June 24, 1932, through a bloodless *coup d'état* led by European-educated intellectuals a constitutional monarchy was founded in Thailand. The principal leaders of this group were Pibul Songgram and Pridi Panomyong. Pibul was the military leader and Pridi was the theorist and administrative head. Phya Bahol, a German-educated colonel, served as liaison between the two, and Phya Manopakorn was appointed the first prime minister. Pridi had an ambitious program for the country. Not only did his People's party promise freedom, equality, and education for the Thai people, it also proposed a thoroughgoing welfare-state socialism. Within a year a secondary coup was executed, the prime ministership was taken by Phya Bahol, and Pridi was exiled on the grounds of "Communistic tendencies." This government remained in power until 1939, when Pibul executed another coup, after which he led the kingdom until 1944. But the year 1935 marks the real end of the absolute monarchy, for in that year King Prajadhipol abdicated the throne and was succeeded by his teenage nephew Ananda. King Ananda, however, was found shot on June 9, 1946, under mysterious circumstances. The present king ascended the throne on May 5, 1950, following a regency.

Under the leadership of Pibul, Thailand gained another distinction. She was the only Southeast Asian nation to join Japan and to declare war against the Allies. During World War II her alliance with Japan at first seemed advantageous as she regained the territories formerly ceded to France and the areas of southern Yunnan, Burma, and Malaya to which she had ethnological links. Yet during the first years of the war the nation suffered greatly from Japanese economic exploitation, and at the war's end she was quickly required to return the new territory.

In 1944 Pibul was replaced by a protégé of Pridi, and in 1946 Pridi took the reins of government in his own hands. During the war he had been associated with the pro-Allies "Free Thai" government. His government was thus quite acceptable, and Thailand became the first of the former enemy to be admitted to the United Nations. Pridi's government, however, was ousted by another coup in 1947. After a short period of civilian rule Pibul, sponsored by the military, was returned to power, and by 1951, as the result of another coup, real power was shifted into the hands of the military with various generals vying for supremacy. Sarit Thanarat was the man who then emerged as the head of the Thai state. In 1958 as commander-in-chief of the army Sarit executed still another coup and became prime minister. He retained this position until his death on December 8, 1963, when Deputy Prime Minister and Defense Minister Thanom Kitlikackorn assumed the post. Thanom seemed to be merely the "front man" for the ruling military oligarchy, and the fear of a new coup hung heavily over the Thai nation. While the army and the police have been almost continually on the alert since Sarit's death, confidence in Thanom's leadership seems in recent months, to be growing, not only because he has survived but also because he himself appears more self-assured than during a brief earlier tenure in power.

Since 1932 six constitutions have been promulgated. Each major shift of power brought about certain changes. The last major constitution, that of 1951, reflects the influence of French and German jurisprudence and of some Anglo-Saxon traditions. It calls for a cabinet-parliamentary system with no true separation of powers, although legislative review is provided by one of the courts. The executive is composed of the king, who exercises no real power, and the Council of Ministers, an appointive group. The Council of Ministers is in fact the ruling body of the country, making policy decisions and nominating one-half the members of the Assembly as well as having the power to issue emergency decrees and to dissolve the Assembly. For the first ten years the Assembly of the

People's Representatives was to be created by the election of one half of its members and the appointment of the other half by the king with the consent of the head of the Council of Ministers. There is, however, a provision which provides for a gradual increase in the number of the elected representatives from each province: as soon as one half of the eligible voters in a province pass the literacy test, the number is increased. Thus after the 1957 election the Assembly was composed of 160 elected members and 123 appointed ones. Although this provision appears to be a progressive step, it should be noted that the ten-year provision expired three years ago. In addition the only real power exercised by the Assembly is its control of the budget. The budget of the previous year remains in effect, however, if the Assembly does not enact a new budget.

In an apt brief analysis of Thai politics David Wilson has commented in *Politics in Thailand:* "The Thai have had little experience with political parties in any form and no experience with the party of mass membership, elaborate organization, and developed ideology. At first the 1932 Promoters called themselves the People's Party but later dropped this name and called their organization a club, which is a precise description of Thai political organizations." Political parties were banned until 1955, except for a brief period from 1945 to 1947. In 1955 upon the passage of the Political Parties Act twenty-three parties came into existence. For the formation of a party a petition signed by five hundred Thai nationals who are eligible voters must be submitted to the Ministry of the Interior. Since the party must be in compliance with section 35 of the constitution, the possibility of a Communist party is eliminated. After the 1957 election only eight parties remained in existence. In actuality there is only one opposition party of any significance, the Prachatipat (Democrat party), which is centered in Bangkok and draws most of its support from the educated middle class and the civil servants. In the past it has stood primarily for civilian control of the military and has called for the end of corruption in the government. In the 1957 elections it won twenty-eight of the elective seats in the Assembly. Thai parties tend to be followers of a personality rather than of an ideology. It should be remembered, however, that Thailand has always been under the control of an oligarchy. Prior to 1932 the oligarchy consisted of the royal family. The coup in that year was not the result of a popular uprising but was in effect the replacement of the royal oligarchy by one composed of civilians and the military. Today the military oligarchy has gained the upper hand, and the electorate is not active.

When the late Marshal Sarit seized power in October 1958, the 1951 constitution was abrogated, the national assembly dissolved, existing political parties disbanded, trade unions closed down, and martial law declared. It has been in effect ever since. The executive power of the Thai state is now vested in the prime minister, the cabinet, and the civil and military bureaucracy. Although power tends to be dispersed throughout the administrative structure, ultimate power rests with the prime minister. The legislative power of the state is nominally vested in a 240-member constituent assembly appointed by royal decree in February 1959. The primary function of this body has been to draft a new constitution. It had been doing this at a very leisurely pace, but the death of Sarit and growing unrest have somewhat accelerated the process.

Unofficially the new draft constitution is reported to provide for a bicameral legislature. The lower house would be elective and would consist of approximately two hundred members. The upper house, or Senate, would be appointed by the king and would consist of 133 members. All legislation would originate in the lower house, with both the Senate and the king possessing a veto power. The nation's chief executive would be the prime minister, who would be appointed by the king after consultation with the presidents of the two legislative chambers. The cabinet would be appointed by the king, without requiring a vote of confidence by the assembly. The king would also be given the power to dissolve the assembly. Assembly deputies could question cabinet ministers and hold general debate on the government without taking a vote.

While a strong tutelary element in the proposed Thai governmental organization is obvious, it is also evident that adoption of this new constitution would represent progress as compared with the present situation in which Thailand is completely under the naked domination of a military clique. Such a trend, if sustained, could result in Thailand's gradual metamorphosis into a genuine Western-style constitutional monarchy. If not, it would merely provide a new façade for a thinly disguised continuation of military rule. When one considers Thai history over the past thirty years, the prognosis for a democratic political development is not too optimistic. But it must be remembered that Thailand has long been accustomed to an authoritarian form of government, and the Thai people have had little experience in self-government. Political parties have existed in Thailand only during three brief periods since World War II. Civilian rule never effectively developed during those periods, and Thai elections have never aroused popular enthusiasm. Only 40 per cent of the people voted in the last free elections, and corruption and fraud were rampant.

On the favorable side it should be noted that the king is young, able, popular, and keenly interested in the welfare of his people. Moreover since World War II there has developed in Thailand a considerable core of Western-educated, reform-minded young leaders and executives such as the minister for national development, Sarasin, and the governor of the Bank of Thailand, Puey, who may constitute the essential nucleus and spearhead of democratic constitutional development in Thailand.

Economic Development

The Thai economy is basically agricultural, with more than 80 per cent of the nation's population deriving their income from this source. Income per capita averages about $100 nationally, but only $60 in the depressed northeast. Rice is the principal Thai crop: it not only feeds the population but also constitutes the major source of export earnings (roughly 33 per cent). The future of rice in the Thai economy is, however, somewhat clouded by declining yields per acre and a rapidly increasing population. Rubber is second in importance, also providing approximately one third of Thai export earnings. The significance of rubber is very much dependent upon fluctuating world prices and increasing competition from the synthetic product. Tin, the third leading Thai export, is similarly dependent on world economic conditions. During the last few years spectacular increases have been recorded among secondary crops like *kenaf* (jute), corn, tobacco, and cotton. Fortunately for political and developmental purposes these crops are suited to the depressed upland areas of the northeast. While there are significant problems and needs in rural Thailand—malaria control, irrigation, water supplies, access roads, and police protection—there is fortunately no serious landlord or rural indebtedness problem in the nation.

Industry still constitutes a small portion of the over-all Thai economy (15 per cent of gross national product in 1961). While the expansion of light, small-scale industry is moving rapidly, there are a number of factors inhibiting private industrial investment, such as small markets, limited power supply, a shortage of local capital, and the overhanging threat of unfair competition from governmental enterprises. The most significant Thai industries include food processing, cement making, sawmilling, tobacco processing, tanneries, and textiles. Thailand suffers from the conventional ills of an underdeveloped, predominantly one-crop economy. This situation results in periodic economic ups and downs, depending on the vagaries of weather and world prices. On the other hand Thailand's growth rate has been extremely favorable, ranging between 4 and 5 per cent during the last decade. Gross fixed investment has been running at about 15 per cent of the gross national product, and a rapid trend toward diversification of the economy has been noted.

Most important, great improvements in Thailand's infrastructure and human resources have been achieved over the past decade, thanks to American and International Bank economic assistance. The nation's highway and railroad systems have been greatly improved and extended. Huge irrigation projects have been undertaken, and electric power capabilities have been vastly increased with the completion of the Yankee multipurpose hydroelectric project. And great progress in the improvement of Thai human resources has been accomplished. A very successful malaria control program has been undertaken throughout the nation. The Thai educational system, both at the primary and secondary levels, has been improved, with special emphasis placed on the development of skilled labor needed for the growing industrial sector of the economy. Considerable assistance has been given to Thailand in the fields of agricultural research and extension, emphasizing diversification of crops, rotation farming, pest control, soil surveys, and the use of fertilizer. As a result of these developments and the great economic progress already achieved in the postwar period, Thailand is now considered to be just short of the so-called "take-off" stage.

Prospects for Development

Thailand has a relatively favorable development potential. Its strong points include fairly rich natural resources in proportion to population, a strong and stable currency which gives confidence to both domestic and foreign investors, an outstanding international credit rating which attracts capital from sources around the world, a tradition of adaptability and social mobility, and a growing cadre of able middle-level administrators. Fortunate in having escaped the distractions of a colonial era and the ravages of World War II, it has also been fortunate in having avoided the serious post–World War II security problems, which would have diverted resources from development, as happened in most other Far Eastern countries. There are, however, significant points of weakness. Thailand has large depressed areas, particularly in the northeast, which are potentially a threat to its political stability. Its educational system needs additional upgrading and overhauling. Private enterprise is still hampered by governmental interference and restrictions. Widespread corruption is more than an annoyance. Most serious of all is mounting Communist pressure in the northeast and continuing friction with Cambodia.

On balance Thailand has good over-all prospects for development. It has a long-standing, well-developed sense of national unity. It is a highly cohesive society, most of whose members are relatively contented Buddhists. Its prospects for economic development appear excellent, both in the short and the long run. Only in the political sphere is the Thai future clouded. The great transition from military feudalism to a society more soundly based on popular consent has not yet been made.

General Thanom, the incumbent prime minister, is perhaps too honest for his own good in a society where corruption is a way of life and everyone expects a share. He served unsuccessfully as prime minister for a brief period in 1958, and he was quickly supplanted by Sarit when the latter returned from a period of convalescence in England. Thanom tends to vacillate and has thus far failed to develop an effective check-and-balance system by which his predecessors maintained power, but his prospects for survival have been improving.

The real power behind the throne appears to be General Praphas, who served as minister of interior under Marshal Sarit and who has recently been given the additional post of commander-in-chief of the Thai army. Praphas has a reputation for being corrupt, having been deeply involved in the Thai "pork monopoly." This image is particularly unfortunate for a major national leader in the wake of the post-mortem scandalous disclosures concerning the late Marshal Sarit, who had amassed a $133 million fortune at what now appears to have been public expense.

Perhaps the greatest threat to Thailand's political stability is that of internal subversion, particularly in the depressed northeastern region. Despite vigorous, high-priority reform programs launched in this area by Marshal Sarit, the Pathet Lao have continued to seep into areas close to the Mekong River. The extent of subversion and Communist penetration of the rank and file in the Thai army is difficult to determine, but at the very least it is not a cause for complacency. The fact that Thai Communists have not yet moved into a state of insurgency is no basis for believing that they lack either the will or the capacity. Equally ominous is Thailand's external political predicament, its relationships to all of its neighbors: Burma, which appears to be falling rapidly under Chinese Communist influence; Laos, weak and torn by civil strife; and hostile Cambodia, whose neutralism is strongly tilting toward Peking. Most serious of all would be the impact of a disaster in South Vietnam.

If the American effort in Vietnam should end in the shock of defeat or in a face-saving settlement like that in Laos, it is possible that Thailand might re-examine the worth of its SEATO and U. S. ties. It might even be tempted to follow Cambodia's neutralist example, which would of course have a profound effect upon the form and path of its future development. This possibility has undoubtedly contributed to the American adoption of a more militant policy in South Vietnam.

SELECTED BIBLIOGRAPHY

INTERNATIONAL BANK FOR RECONSTRUCTION AND DEVELOPMENT. *A Public Development Program for Thailand.* Baltimore: Johns Hopkins Press, 1959.

LANDON, K. P. *Siam in Transition.* Chicago, Ill.: Univ. of Chicago Press, 1939.

MOSEL, JAMES. "Thai Administrative Behavior," in *Toward the Comparative Study of Public Administration,* ed. William J. Sifflin. Bloomington, Ind.: Indiana Univ. Department of Government, 1957.

PICKERELL, ALBERT, and D. E. MOORE. "Elections in Thailand," *Far Eastern Survey,* XXVI (1957), 92–96, 103–111.

REEVE, W. D. *Public Administrations in Siam.* London: Royal Institute of International Affairs, 1951.

SKINNER, G. W. *Leadership and Power in the Chinese Community of Thailand,* Ithaca, N.Y.: Cornell Univ. Press, 1958.

THOMPSON, VIRGINIA, and RICHARD ADLOFF. "The State's Role in Thai Economy," *Far Eastern Survey,* XXI (1952), 123–27.

WARNER, DENIS. "Aggressions by Seepage in the Northeast," *The Reporter,* October 25, 1962, 33–37.

WILSON, D. A. *Politics in Thailand.* Ithaca, N.Y.: Cornell Univ. Press, 1962.

———. "Thailand," in *Governments and Politics of Southeast Asia,* ed. G. McT. Kahin. 2nd edn., Ithaca, N.Y.: Cornell Univ. Press, 1964.

915 y F.W.